CAMPAIGN 381

BATTLE OF MALTA

June 1940–November 1942

ANTHONY ROGERS   ILLUSTRATED BY GRAHAM TURNER

Series editor Nikolai Bogdanovic

OSPREY PUBLISHING
Bloomsbury Publishing Plc
Kemp House, Chawley Park, Cumnor Hill, Oxford OX2 9PH, UK
29 Earlsfort Terrace, Dublin 2, Ireland
1385 Broadway, 5th Floor, New York, NY 10018, USA
E-mail: info@ospreypublishing.com
www.ospreypublishing.com

OSPREY is a trademark of Osprey Publishing Ltd

First published in Great Britain in 2022

A catalogue record for this book is available from the British Library.

ISBN: PB 9781472848901; eBook 9781472848871; ePDF 9781472848895;
XML 9781472848888

22 23 24 25 26   10 9 8 7 6 5 4 3 2 1

Maps by Bounford.com
3D BEVs by Paul Kime
Index by Zoe Ross
Typeset by PDQ Digital Media Solutions, Bungay, UK
Printed and bound in India by Replika Press Private Ltd.

Artist's note

Readers may care to note that the original paintings from which the colour
plates in this book were prepared are available for private sale. All
reproduction copyright whatsoever is retained by the publishers. All
enquiries should be addressed to:
Graham Turner, PO Box 568, Aylesbury, Bucks. HP17 8ZX UK
www.studio88.co.uk
The publishers regret that they can enter into no correspondence upon
this matter.

Photographs

The images in this work are from the author's collection, unless
otherwise indicated.

Osprey Publishing supports the Woodland Trust, the UK's leading woodland
conservation charity.

To find out more about our authors and books visit
www.ospreypublishing.com. Here you will find extracts, author
interviews, details of forthcoming events and the option to sign up for
our newsletter.

Author's acknowledgements

Thank you to all who helped during the preparation of this work. From
Germany, Hans Peter Eisenbach and Peter Schenk provided German
reference material, all of which was kindly translated by Bettina Selke.
Ludovico Slongo, in Italy, clarified Italian air operations. Further assistance
was forthcoming from Jeff Sammut, David Bartolo and Charles Debono
in Malta.

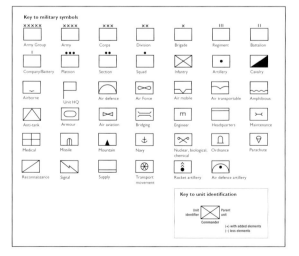

Front cover main illustration: A Stuka dive-bombing attack on the
Grand Harbour. (Graham Turner)

Title page photograph: A low-flying Ju 88 over Għadira, Malta,
probably on 25 April 1942.

CONTENTS

INTRODUCTION 5

CHRONOLOGY 7

OPPOSING COMMANDERS 9
British . Axis

OPPOSING FORCES 14
British . Axis

OPPOSING PLANS 19

THE BATTLE 23
Start of the air war . First naval surface engagements . Operation 'Hurry' . Malta Convoys
Operation 'Excess' and the '*Illustrious* Blitz' . Messerschmitt Bf 109s join battle . Spring–summer, 1941
Italian seaborne attack on Grand Harbour . Autumn, 1941 . Destruction of the '*Maestrale*' Convoy
Early U-boat operations . Return of the Luftwaffe . *Schnellboot* operations . Spitfires join battle
'M.W.10' . April, 1942 . '*C3*'/'*Herkules*' . May, 1942 . 3.Schnellbootflottille . Axis clandestine operations
Operation 'Julius' . Operation 'Pedestal' . Autumn 1942 and the final Axis offensive

SUMMARY 89

THE BATTLEFIELD TODAY 91

ACRONYMS AND ABBREVIATIONS 93

BIBLIOGRAPHY 94

INDEX 95

The Mediterranean in June 1940

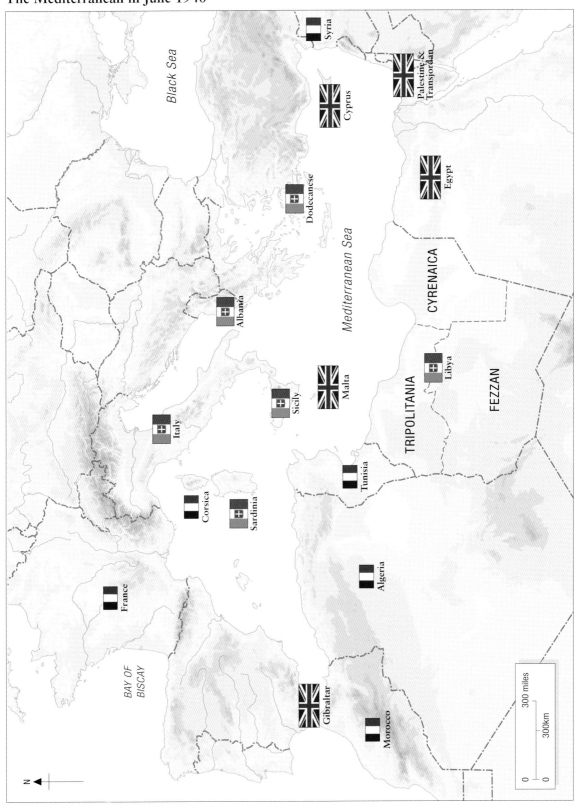

Black Sea

Syria

Palestine &
Transjordan

Cyprus

Egypt

Dodecanese

Mediterranean Sea

CYRENAICA

Albania

Libya

Malta

TRIPOLITANIA

FEZZAN

Sicily

Italy

Tunisia

Corsica

Sardinia

Algeria

France

BAY OF
BISCAY

Gibraltar

Morocco

N

300 miles

300km

0

0

INTRODUCTION

At just 17½ miles by 8¼ (approximately 28 x 13km), Malta is the largest of two inhabited islands, the other being Gozo just to the north. In-between is tiny Comino. Filfla and other uninhabited islets complete the archipelago, which is situated in the middle of the Mediterranean, some 55 miles (88.5km) south of Sicily and almost equidistant from Gibraltar in the far-off western approaches and Suez in the east.

Today, Malta is a popular holiday destination, but in times past, it was a valued strategic location. The island had been settled by the Phoenicians, Carthaginians and, in the 2nd century BC, the Romans. After several hundred years under the Byzantines, there followed more than 200 years of Arab rule, subsequent to the arrival of the Normans towards the end of the 11th century. The Maltese Islands joined the Kingdom of Sicily and in 1530 were granted by Charles V to the Knights Hospitaller, following their defeat and banishment from Rhodes by the Ottomans. In 1565, the Ottomans attempted, and failed, to seize Malta during a four-month siege. Thereafter, Malta was ruled by the Knights until 1798 and the unwelcome occupation by French troops. Two years later, British forces were instrumental in ousting the French. This brought about a request by Malta for Britain to assume sovereignty of the islands. In 1814, Malta joined the British Empire to

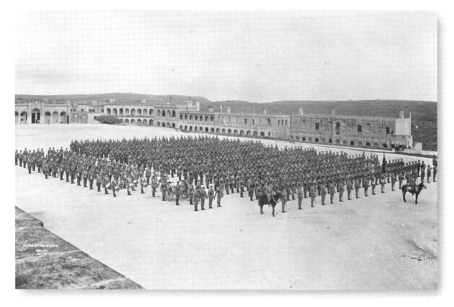

Malta was an important strategic outpost for the British Armed Forces, with military bases situated throughout the island. In this pre-war image, an unidentified battalion parades at Imtarfa Barracks.

become an important base for the Royal Navy, the British Army and, more than a century later, the Royal Air Force (RAF).

As a Crown Colony, there were advantages. But there was also a real risk of becoming embroiled in Britain's wars. Malta escaped the ravages suffered by much of Europe during the First World War, when the island served as an essential medical centre for battle casualties evacuated from the Dardanelles and elsewhere. During the Second World War, however, it would be an entirely different situation.

Malta had been the subject of debate even before the commencement of hostilities. The British Admiralty favoured the strengthening of the island. The Air Ministry was less enthusiastic, considering the risks posed by the proximity of Italian airfields. In the event, Britain's Committee of Imperial Defence agreed to increase Malta's defences. It was planned to improve existing anti-aircraft (AA) capabilities and also took into account the requirement for fighter aircraft. Malta was already equipped with the first radio direction finding (RDF, or radar) station outside the United Kingdom. There was an established airfield at Ħal Far in the south-east and a centrally-located civil airport at Ta' Qali (soon to be commandeered for military use). Construction of a sizeable airfield near Luqa in central-eastern Malta was also underway. In addition, there was a seaplane station not far from Ħal Far at Kalafrana, and seaplane facilities at nearby Marsaxlokk and towards the north-west at St Paul's Bay.

But when, on 10 June 1940, Italy entered the war against Britain and France, Malta was far from being prepared. Luqa airfield had yet to become operational. Anti-aircraft capabilities were lacking. Crucially, there was no fighter defence, other than several Royal Navy Gloster Sea Gladiators recently taken over by the RAF.

Six Gladiators are known to have been on strength at various times. These are N5520, N5524 and N5529 at Luqa airfield in late summer or autumn of 1940.

CHRONOLOGY

1940

10 June	Italy declares war on Britain and France.
11 June	Units of the Regia Aeronautica commence air operations against Malta.
21–22 June	First Hurricanes reach Malta.
12 August	Conclusion of Operation 'Hurry', first naval operation to ferry Hurricanes by aircraft carrier to within flying range of Malta.
2 September	Arrival of the first inbound Malta convoy ('M.F.2') with RFA *Plumleaf* and supply ships *Cornwall* and *Volo*.
11 October	Four supply ships reach Malta ('M.F.3').
28 October	Italy invades Greece and, soon after, British forces move to defend Crete.
9 November	Five supply ships reach Malta ('M.W.3').
17 November	Operation 'White' – five Hurricanes arrive at Malta (eight are lost).
26 November	Four supply ships reach Malta ('M.W.4').
28 November	Two supply ships reach Malta ('Collar').
20 December	Seven supply ships reach Malta ('M.W.5A' and 'M.W.5B').

1941

10 January	First operations in the central Mediterranean by X.Fliegerkorps. Three supply ships reach Malta ('M.W.5½' and 'Excess').
16–19 January	Heavy air attacks by X.Fliegerkorps on the aircraft carrier HMS *Illustrious* in Grand Harbour.
21 February	1st Battalion The Cheshire Regiment and 1st Battalion The Hampshire Regiment arrive by sea from Alexandria ('M.C.8').
23 March	Four supply ships reach Malta ('M.W.6').
6 April	Yugoslavia invaded by German-led forces.
9 May	Five supply ships and two tankers reach Malta ('M.W.7A' and 'M.W.7B').

Mid-May	Some Luftwaffe units in Sicily are redeployed to other fronts.
20 May	German forces invade Crete.
6–30 June	Reinforcement of Malta's fighter units (operations 'Rocket', 'Tracer', 'Railway I' and 'Railway II').
25/26 July	Attack by MAS X on Grand Harbour.
24 July	Six supply ships reach Malta ('G.M.1').
28 September	Eight supply ships reach Malta ('G.M.2').
December	II.Fliegerkorps is ordered to Sicily.
16/17 December	3.Schnellbootflottille commence mining operations off Malta.

1942

19 January	Three supply ships reach Malta ('M.W.8A' and 'M.W.8B').
7 March	First Spitfires arrive (Operation 'Spotter').
22 March 1942	Second Battle of Sirte.
23 March	*Breconshire* and two supply ships reach Malta ('M.W.10').
15 April	Malta is awarded the George Cross.
29–30 April	Hitler apparently sanctions an Italo-German invasion of Malta, (codename 'C3' by the Italians and '*Herkules*' by the Germans).
Early May	Some Luftwaffe units are redeployed from Sicily.
18 May	Mining operations off Malta by 3.Schnellbootflottille are suspended.
10 June	Two supply ships reach Malta ('G.M.4'); a second convoy ('M.W.11') does not get through.
22 June	Hitler postpones '*Herkules*' until at least the end of August, effectively terminating the operation.
15 August	Arrival at Grand Harbour of oil tanker *Ohio* (Operation 'Pedestal').
11–18 October	Last major Axis blitz ends in failure for Italo-German forces.
3–5 November	3.Schnellbootflottille undertakes last three mining operations off Malta.
20 November	Operation 'Stoneage' and arrival of all four supply ships ('M.W.13') effectively brings an end to the siege of Malta.

OPPOSING COMMANDERS

BRITISH

In May 1940, **Lieutenant-General (Later Sir) William G. S. Dobbie** took over from an ailing **General Sir Charles Bonham-Carter** to become (initially acting) Governor and Commander-in-Chief (C-in-C) of Malta. Dobbie had been commissioned as a second lieutenant in the Royal Engineers in August 1899, seeing active service in the Boer War. In 1914 he joined the British Expeditionary Force and served in France and Belgium. He remained on the General Staff for much of the First World War, rising to the rank of brevet lieutenant-colonel by 1917. Subsequently, he served with the Rhine Army before being posted back to Britain. Thereafter, he was rapidly promoted. Between June 1928 and July 1932, he was a brigade commander in Egypt before returning to Britain for several years. In November 1935 he was appointed General Officer Commanding (GOC) British Forces in Malaya. This was to have been his final posting before retiring in August 1939. However, the Second World War provided Dobbie with an opportunity to again serve his country, when he was despatched to take charge at Malta. Two years later, in May 1942, Dobbie was succeeded by **John Standish Surtees Prendergast Vereker, 6th Viscount Gort**. Lord Gort was commissioned as a second lieutenant in the Grenadier Guards in August 1905. During the First World War, he saw action on the Western Front. In September 1918, the then-Acting Lieutenant Colonel led an attack near Flesquieres, for which he was awarded the Victoria Cross. Gort enjoyed a varied post-war career, both in Britain and overseas, being promoted to major general in November 1935. Just two years later, on 6 December 1937, he became a General and at the same time was appointed Chief of the Imperial General Staff. After the outbreak of the Second World War, Gort commanded the British Expeditionary Force, overseeing the 1940 evacuation from Dunkirk. A home posting followed, during which he was appointed ADC (Aide-de-

Governor and Commander-in-Chief (C-in-C), Malta, at the outbreak of the Second World War was General (later Sir) William Dobbie (right), seen here with the Prime Minister of the Polish Government in Exile, General Władysław Sikorski. (Charles Debono/National War Museum)

In May 1942, Dobbie was succeeded as Malta's Governor and C-in-C by Lord Gort.

Camp) General to King George VI. In May 1941, Lord Gort became Governor and C-in-C of Gibraltar prior to taking over from Dobbie at Malta a year later, and remaining until September 1944.

Vice Admiral (later Sir) Wilbraham T. R. Ford. had joined the Royal Navy as a cadet in 1894. After the First World War, in which he served as a commander, Ford was promoted to captain. Between the wars he commanded warships and shore establishments, rising to the rank of rear admiral in November 1932. He commanded His Majesty's Australian Squadron for two years (April 1934 to April 1936) before becoming Vice Admiral-in-Charge, Malta, and Admiral Superintendent, Malta Dockyard in January 1937. On 1 January 1942, he handed over to **Vice Admiral Sir Ralph Leatham.** He had also joined the Royal Navy as a cadet, rising to the rank of commander before the end of the First World War. He held senior appointments both onshore and at sea during the inter-war period and in June 1938 was appointed Rear-Admiral 1st Battle Squadron. At the start of the Second World War, he was a newly promoted vice admiral and C-in-C East Indies Station, subsequent to taking over from Vice Admiral Ford as Flag Officer-in-Charge, Malta, until the end of the island siege.

Major-General (later Sir) S. J. P. (John) Scobell had joined the Norfolk Regiment as a second lieutenant in August 1899. He was a lieutenant in the Somaliland campaign and, during the First World War, saw active service at the Western front, attaining the rank of brevet lieutenant colonel in January 1918. Between the wars Scobell served overseas as Chief of Staff (CoS) of the Military Mission to Russia, at the Black Sea and in Turkey. After a spell at the War Office as Assistant Adjutant General (AAG), he was posted to India as Commandant, Senior Officers School at Belgaum, subsequent to being appointed as a brigade commander and, eventually, Commander of Bombay District. In October 1939, Scobell was appointed GOC Troops, Malta, a post he retained until 6 January 1942. He was succeeded by **Colonel (Acting Major-General) Daniel M. W. Beak.** Beak had joined the Royal Naval Volunteer Reserve (RNVR) as a rating in February 1915. He was soon commissioned. During the First World War he was employed essentially in an infantry role, seeing active service at Gallipoli, France and Belgium. For his role at Logeast Wood, near Bapaume, during August and September 1918, Beak, by this time a commander (temporary) leading Drake Battalion, was awarded the Victoria Cross. He returned to civilian life in June 1919, but in 1921 joined the regular army as a captain in the Royal Scots Fusiliers. During the 1930s, Beak was steadily promoted. He twice transferred, first to the King's Regiment (Liverpool) and then to the South Lancashire Regiment (The Prince of Wales's Volunteers), seeing action in France in May 1940 as a battalion commander. Beak went on to command 12th Infantry Brigade subsequent to arriving at Malta. After his departure, on 14 July 1942, the Commander Royal Artillery Malta, **Colonel (Acting Major-General) Clifford T. Beckett,** took on the role of GOC for three weeks subsequent to the arrival of **Major-General Ronald MacK. Scobie.** Commissioned as a second lieutenant in the Royal Engineers in February 1914, Scobie saw active service on the Western Front, finishing the war as a captain. Between the wars he served both at home and overseas. On the outbreak of the Second World War he was Deputy Director of Mobilization and in the following year was posted to the Middle East, serving as a senior staff officer until October 1941, when he became GOC of 70th Division, taking over command of troops in and around Tobruk. In 1942, Scobie was reappointed as Deputy Adjutant-General (DAG), Middle East, subsequent to arriving at Malta in August, where he was GOC until March 1943.

Malta's military commanders photographed at the presentation ceremony of the George Cross on 13 September 1942. From left: Air Vice-Marshal (soon to be Sir) Keith Park, Vice Admiral Sir Ralph Leatham and Major-General R. Mack. Scobie.

Air Commodore Forster H. M. Maynard was Air Officer Commanding (AOC), RAF Mediterranean at the outbreak of war with Italy. His military service began in October 1912, when he joined Leeds University Officers' Training Corps. Two years later, he enlisted in the Royal Naval Divisional Engineers, but in May 1915 embarked on a very different career path. He was commissioned in the Royal Naval Air Service (RNAS), later to merge with the Royal Flying Corps (RFC) to form the Royal Air Force, seeing action on the Western Front as a fighter pilot. By the end of the war he was a captain (acting major) in the RAF. In August 1938, and by this time a Group Captain, Maynard was appointed Deputy Director Staff Duties, Assistant Chief of the Air Staff. Promotion to temporary Air Commodore followed in January 1940, together with a posting to Malta whereupon he assumed command from **Air Commodore Robert Leckie.** Maynard was promoted to acting Air Vice-Marshal on 14 February 1941 and on 1 June was succeeded as AOC at Malta by **Air Vice-Marshal Hugh Pughe Lloyd.** During the First World War Lloyd had enlisted as a pioneer in the Royal Engineers, serving as a despatch rider on the Western Front. In 1917 he was granted a commission in the RFC, qualifying as a pilot and seeing further action, this time flying army cooperating missions. After the war he served in the RAF both at home and in India. He was steadily promoted, and during the first years of the Second World War rose from Wing Commander to become acting Air Vice-Marshal concurrent with his posting to Malta. Lloyd was succeeded in July 1942 by **Air Vice-Marshal (later Sir) Keith R. Park.** Park had served as an enlisted man in the New Zealand Howitzer Brigade at Gallipoli in 1915. In September he was commissioned as a second lieutenant in the Royal Horse and Field Artillery of the British Army, and remained at Gallipoli until the Allied withdrawal. In October 1916, while serving on the Western Front, he was wounded and evacuated to Britain. He obtained a commission in the RFC in December 1916 and saw further action piloting the Bristol F.2 Fighter. Park remained in the RAF and was appointed Air ADC to the

King in January 1937. After a few months as Officer Commanding (OC) RAF Tangmere, he was employed as Senior Air Staff Officer at Fighter Command, subsequent to taking over as AOC No. 11 Group, Fighter Command (April–December 1940) and then as AOC No. 23 Group (December 1940–January 1942). After a period as AOC in Egypt, Park was posted to Malta, remaining as AOC until his departure in January 1944.

AXIS

Italian

Generale Gennaro Tedeschini Lalli served as a junior officer in Italy's Regio Esercito (Royal Army). He saw active service in the 1911–12 Italo-Turkish War and the First World War, at which time he transferred to the army's aviation branch, Corpo Aeronautico Militare, forerunner of the Regia Aeronautica – the Italian Royal Air Force – and was assigned to airships. During the 1930s he held several command posts, including as head of *Comando Aeronautica dell'Africa Orientale italiana* (Air Force Command of Italian East Africa), before a home posting to take charge of 2ª Squadra Aerea in Sicily. In January 1941, he was succeeded by **Generale Renato Mazzucco**, a fighter squadriglia commander in the First World War. In-between the wars he held various staff appointments and also acquired a reputation as a sports flier, winning *La Coppa Barracca* in 1922 and 1923. Prior to the appointment of Lalli, he was head of the air force in East Africa. At the end of 1941, Mazzucco handed over command of 2ª Squadra Aerea to **Silvio Scaroni**. This former artillery NCO in the Italian army had transferred to the Corpo Aeronautico Militare in March 1915. He qualified as a reconnaissance pilot, was commissioned in 1917 and transferred to fighters. By the end of the First World War, Scaroni was Italy's second highest-scoring fighter pilot. Between the wars he was stationed at home and overseas, including as Italy's Air Attaché in Britain and, subsequently, the United States. In the mid-1930s, he led the Regia Aeronautica military mission in China. On the eve of Italy's declaration of war, in June 1940, Scaroni commanded 2ª Divisione Aerea Caccia Terrestre 'Borea' (1ª Squadra Aerea). As *generale di divisione aerea* he would hold a number of key posts, among them commander of the Regia Aeronautica in Sicily from December 1941 to December 1943.

German

Albert Kesselring joined the army as an officer cadet in 1904 and was commissioned in a Bavarian artillery regiment. He was on both the Western and Eastern Fronts during the First World War, at the end of which he continued to serve as an artillery officer. He was seconded to the Reichswehr in October 1922 and was instrumental in its development as the future Wehrmacht – the German armed forces. Towards the end of 1933 he was discharged from the Reichswehr to become head of the Department of Administration at the *Reichskommissariat für die Luftfahrt* (Reich Commissariat for Aviation) with the rank of *Oberst*. In June 1936, then Generalleutnant Kesselring was appointed CoS of the Luftwaffe (the Air Force, established the previous year) and from mid-1937 until late-

In November 1941, Generalfeldmarschall Albert Kesselring became Wehrmacht C-in-C South, assuming responsibility for operations in the Mediterranean theatre.

September 1938 commanded Luftkreis III in Dresden, before taking charge of Luftflotte 1 in Berlin. After the invasion of Poland and prior to the invasion of the Netherlands and the Battle of France, he took over Luftflotte 2 from General der Flieger Hellmuth Felmy. Promoted to *Generalfeldmarschall* in July 1940, Kesselring continued to command Luftflotte 2 in the Battle of Britain and Operation 'Barbarossa'. In November 1941, Kesselring was appointed Wehrmacht C-in-C South, with responsibility for operations in the Mediterranean theatre.

In December 1941, II.Fliegerkorps under General der Flieger Hans Ferdinand Geisler (right) joined the Italian air force in its air campaign against Malta. (Bundesarchiv, Bild 101I-422-0034-29)

Hans Ferdinand Geisler began his military service in the Imperial German Navy, joining in 1909 as an officer cadet. He remained in the navy until 1933, when he transferred to the *Luftschutzamt*. In September 1939, then Generalleutnant Geisler took command of 10.Flieger-Division, soon to be re-designated X.Fliegerkorps. Promoted to *General der Flieger* in July 1940, Geisler continued to head X.Fliegerkorps during Malta air operations for the first half of 1941.

Pre-1914, **Bruno Loerzer** was an army officer before joining the air force and becoming a reconnaissance pilot (when the future Reichsmarschall, Hermann Göring, flew as his observer). He later transferred to fighters to become one of Germany's top-scoring aces of the First World War. After a period as *Inspekteur der Jagdflieger* (Inspector of Fighters) he was appointed commander of 2.Flieger-Division in February 1939 subsequent to its reorganization as II.Fliegerkorps, which, in December 1941, became responsible for neutralizing Malta under Loerzer, now a *Generalleutnant*. In July 1942, Loerzer was promoted to *General der Flieger*.

X.Fliegerkorps, responsible for Luftwaffe air operations against Malta during 1942, was commanded by Generalleutnant Bruno Loerzer (right), seen here with *Il Duce* Benito Mussolini and Reichsmarschall Hermann Göring. (Bundesarchiv, Bild 146-1979-155-18)

OPPOSING FORCES

BRITISH

For members of the British armed forces, pre-war Malta provided an enviable life-style. As a former officer in the Queen's Own would recall, 'Malta was one of the finest peace-time stations one could wish for.' Officers, often accompanied by their families, were provided with spacious houses in the best residential areas and enjoyed a busy social life. For other ranks (ORs), life was comfortable, if less glamorous than that of the officer class. Unaccompanied ORs were accommodated in barracks, the largest of which was Pembroke, constructed in the mid-19th century on the northern coast. There were also army establishments at Mtarfa, in central Malta, and on the north-western coast at Għajn Tuffieħa.

In the months following the outbreak of the Second World War, life continued very much as before. But some doubted whether it was practical or even possible for Malta to remain a Crown Colony and plans to improve the island's defences took time to implement.

Malta is an island of walled cities and fortifications. Distributed between ten forts were 9.2-inch and 6-inch guns and quick-firing 6-pdrs.

At the start of the siege of Malta in 1940, there were on the island six British and three Maltese infantry battalions. Before the siege was lifted, these had increased to 15 battalions. These are men of 4 Buffs in 1941.

By June 1940, Malta had been provided with just 34 heavy anti-aircraft (HAA) guns and eight Bofors light anti-aircraft (LAA) guns. These were also 24 searchlights. At the height of the battle, in May 1942, there would be 31 HAA gun sites totalling 12 4.5-inch, 80 3.7-inch and 20 3-inch guns; LAA guns were dispersed at 136 sites. 18-pdr and 25-pdr field guns were also situated at various locations.

In June 1940, there was on Malta little in the way of an air force. However, a number of

Malta was defended by light anti-aircraft (LAA) and heavy anti-aircraft (HAA) guns. These men of the Royal Artillery are from 32nd LAA Regiment. Steel helmets, and other equipment, are painted in the distinctive 'rubble wall' camouflage pattern unique to Malta-based personnel.

Gloster Sea Gladiator biplanes, disassembled and in storage crates, had been assigned by the Navy to the RAF. Four were made ready and, with the seven RAF pilots who would fly them, based initially at Ḥal Far, before relocating in late June 1940 to Luqa. Malta's Gladiators were soon joined by Hawker Hurricane Mk Is, with fighter pilots posted from the UK. Hurricane Is and IIs would continue to arrive until, in March 1942, fighter squadrons began to re-equip with Supermarine Spitfire Vs. These would eventually replace the Hurricane altogether. During 1940–42, Malta also served as a base for bombers, long-range fighters and reconnaissance machines, including the Vickers Wellington, Bristol Beaufighter, Bristol Blenheim, Bristol Beaufort, Glenn Martin 167 (Maryland), Blackburn Skua, Fairey Swordfish, Fairey Fulmar and Fairey Albacore.

In the mid-1930s Malta had been provided with an early warning system when Royal Engineers constructed a Parabolic Acoustic Mirror at Ta' San Pietru. This became redundant in March 1939 following the arrival of one of the first radar stations from Britain. This was erected near

Without the Royal Air Force and the senior service – the Royal Navy – Malta could not have survived. This photograph was taken on board HMS *Argus* at Gibraltar in July 1940, during Operation 'Hurry', the first attempt to reinforce Malta with fighters from an aircraft carrier. The sergeant pilot in shirtsleeves is thought to be Roy O'Donnell, who was shot down and killed just two weeks after this picture was taken. To his right is Sergeant W. J. (Bill) Timms, who lost his life as a result of a low-level bale-out from his Hurricane on 11 January 1941.

Infantry sectors in May/June 1940

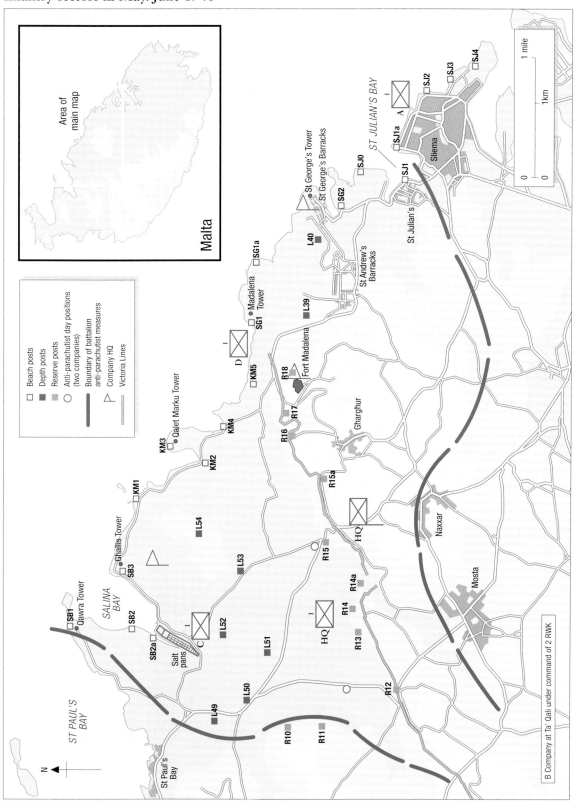

Area of main map

Malta

Legend:
- □ Beach posts
- ■ Depth posts
- ▓ Reserve posts
- ⊠ Anti-parachutist day positions (two companies)
- ⦵ Boundary of battalion anti-parachutist measures
- ○ Company HQ
- △ Victoria Lines

ST PAUL'S BAY

St Paul's Bay

SALINA BAY

Qawra Tower

SB1
SB2a
SB2
Salt pans
C
SB3
Ghallis Tower

L54
L53
L52
L51
L50
L49

R10
R11
R12
R13
R14
R14a
R15
R15a
HQ

KM1
KM2
KM3
KM4
KM5
Qalet Marku Tower

D

SG1
SG1a
Madalena Tower
KM5
R18
Fort Madalena
R17
R16

L40
L39

Gharghur

St George's Tower
St George's Barracks
SG2
SG1a

St Andrew's Barracks

SJ0
SJ1
SJ1a
A
SJ2
SJ3
SJ4

St Julian's

ST JULIAN'S BAY

Sliema

Naxxar

Mosta

HQ

N

1 mile
1km
0
0

B Company at Ta' Qali under command of 2 RWK

Dingli, the island's highest point on the southern coast. Additional Air Ministry Experimental Stations (AMES) would arrive in due course.

In June 1940, there were five British and three Maltese infantry battalions dispersed at various locations, plus units of the **Royal Artillery, Royal Malta Artillery** and, at Fort St Angelo, a detachment of the **Royal Marines**. Infantry manned pillboxes, beach and defence posts and would later assist at airfields and in the unloading of supply ships. By late-1942, Malta's land forces had increased substantially and would include 11 British and four Maltese infantry battalions. By late 1940 there was also a troop of the **Royal Armoured Corps** equipped with four Infantry Mk II (Matilda) and two Light Mk VI (Vickers) tanks.

Malta was an important base for the Royal Navy, not least because of the excellent port facilities at Grand Harbour. These are Fleet Air Arm (FAA) torpedo bomber crews. FAA Albacores operated out of Ħal Far airfield, which the navy shared with the Royal Air Force.

Among support elements were **Royal Engineers, Royal Corps of Signals, Royal Army Ordnance Corps, Royal Army Service Corps, Royal Army Pay Corps** and **Corps of Military Police**. The **Royal Army Medical Corps** played a vital role and in 1940 was responsible for No. 90 British General Hospital at Mtarfa. At Pembroke in late 1941, two more hospitals were made ready: No. 39 on the coast below St Andrew's Barracks and No. 45 at nearby St Patrick's Barracks. In early 1941, Numbers 15 and 161 Field Ambulance also commenced operations.

Initially, Malta was divided into infantry defence sectors. In August 1940, **1 Infantry Brigade** became responsible for southern Malta and **2 Infantry Brigade** was established to cover the northern region. They would later be supplemented with 3 (Central) and 4 (Western) Infantry brigades.

The **Royal Navy** remained active throughout the siege. Submarines operated from their base at Lazzaretto (Manoel Island) and destroyers from Grand Harbour. Warships came and went, making use of port facilities in order to refuel and, if necessary, repair. Warships of the Mediterranean Fleet, based at Alexandria, Egypt, and of Force H, based at Gibraltar, would be absolutely essential in protecting merchant ships during Malta convoys.

Initially, Axis air operations were the responsibility of the Italian Air Force. These air mechanics of 259ª Squadriglia, 109º Gruppo, 36º Stormo bombardamento terrestre (B.T.) are seen at Castelvetrano, Sicily, in November 1940.

AXIS

In June 1940, the Regia Aeronautica was considered to be a modern, well-equipped branch of the Italian military. When Italy's *Il Duce*, Benito Mussolini, declared war, Malta became a primary objective, with air operations undertaken initially by 2ª Squadra Aerea, based

In January 1941, the Italians were joined in their offensive against Malta by X.Fliegerkorps of the German Air Force. In February, 7.Staffel of Jagdgeschwader 26 commenced fighter operations over the island. This group includes, from left: Unteroffizier Wagner, Oberfeldwebel Karl Kühdorf (wearing peak cap), unknown, Leutnant Hans Johannsen (on elbow), Oberfeldwebel Ernst Laube, unknown, Unteroffizier Karl-Heinz Ehlen and Unteroffizier Georg Mondry. The two on the far-right are Oberleutnant Klaus Mietusch and (wearing sunglasses) Feldwebel Leibling.

on Sicily and comprising 1ª Divisione Aerea (equipped with Fiat CR.42 and Macchi C.200 fighters), 3ª Divisione Aerea (Savoia S.79 'Sparviero' bombers) and 11ª Divisione Aerea (SIAI S.79 and S.85 bombers). Also available were CRDA Cant. Z.501 and Z.506B flying boats and reconnaissance IMAM Ro.37 bis. As the war continued, more and often-better Italian machines were employed, among them the Macchi C.202 and Reggiane Re.2001, Cant Z.1007bis, Fiat BR.20M and SIAI S.84. Main airfields were situated near the Sicilian capital at Palermo on the north-western coast; in the east at Trapani, Castelvetrano and Sciacca; at Gela and Comiso in the south-east and at Catania on the eastern coast. The western Mediterranean was covered by *Aeronautica della Sardegna* (Sardinia) and the east by *Aeronautica dell' Egeo*, with its headquarters on Rhodes. As with the RAF on Malta, operational requirements would result in a constant coming and going of air force units and an order of battle that was ever-changing.[1]

Towards the end of 1940, elements of X.Fliegerkorps of the Luftwaffe began to arrive in Sicily and for several months all but replaced the Regia Aeronautica in the skies over and around Malta. By January 1941, the Italian air force on Sicily came under *Comando Aeronautica Sicilia*, with its headquarters at Palermo. When, in mid-1941, X.Fliegerkorps was redeployed, Malta once more became the responsibility of the Italians. At the end of the year, the Luftwaffe returned, this time with II.Fliegerkorps.

The Luftwaffe primary medium bomber during Malta operations was the Junkers Ju 88 (as with all aircraft types, improved variants came into service as the war continued). The Ju 87 'Stuka' dive-bomber and Messerschmitt Bf 110 heavy fighter were both used until mid-1942, by which time the Spitfire had replaced the Hurricane, exposing the vulnerability of these aircraft. The Messerschmitt Bf 109 was introduced into the battle in February 1941 and used extensively to escort bombers, in fighter sweeps and as a fighter-bomber.

The Battle of Malta, although primarily an air war, also involved Axis naval units, notably the Italian special operations Xª Flottiglia MAS and the German 3.Schnellbootflottille, the latter equipped with motor torpedo boats (known to the Allies as E-Boats). Axis submarines and the Regia Marina (Italian Royal Navy) were another ever-present threat, although, as will be seen, Italian warships were not always employed to their full advantage.

1   For further details about Italian and German air force units see Ryan K. Noppen, *Malta 1940–42: The Axis' Air Battle for Mediterranean Supremacy* (No. 4 in the Osprey Air Campaign series).

OPPOSING PLANS

In the early 20th century, North Africa and much of the Middle East had been claimed by various European powers. Italy dominated Libya and Somalia, Eritrea and the Ethiopian Empire. Vichy France occupied most of the vast north-western region: Tunisia, Algeria, French Morocco and French West Africa, as well as Cameroon further south. Britain controlled territory stretching from Sierra Leone, on Africa's west coast, the Gold Coast and Nigeria and east to Sudan, Egypt, Palestine and beyond. Italy's entry into the war therefore posed a threat to Britain's position not only on Malta, but also in the Middle East, jeopardising oil supplies and access to and from India and the Far East via the Suez Canal.

Malta was bombed within hours of Italy's declaration of war. In the meantime, Allied aircraft bombed bases in Italian East Africa and later that night British bombers targeted Turin and Genoa in Italy. In North Africa, British troops entered Libya from Egypt, clashing with Italian forces and taking a number of prisoners. It was the start of the Desert War, which continued for nearly three years and with which Malta would be inextricably linked. During the first few months, the Italians fared badly, steadily losing ground to British Commonwealth and Dominion forces. This did not prevent

For as long as Malta held out, the island represented a potent threat to Axis Mediterranean supply lines. At Ħal Far, a Fleet Air Arm Albacore is armed with a torpedo in preparation for a shipping strike.

If Malta were to be captured, it first had to be neutralized. Primary objectives included airfields. This is Hal Far, on the south-eastern coast, as seen from the cockpit of a Ju 87 in 1941. (Bundesarchiv, Bild Bild 101I-422-0044-27)

Luqa airfield, developed to accommodate twin-engine machines, such as Wellington bombers, also provided a base for fighters. There were four runways. Aircraft hangars can be seen at the north-west end of the north-west to south-east runway. The north to south runway extends to right of frame, crossing the east to west runway. The north-east end of the north-east to south-west runway can also be seen. This photograph was taken from a Hurricane in early 1941.

Mussolini from seeking to expand his country's influence elsewhere. On 28 October 1940, Italian forces invaded Greece, only to meet with determined resistance and having to withdraw into neighbouring Albania.

Events in Libya, the Italian failure in Greece and potential threat to German oil supplies in Romania, and ineffectual Italian air attacks on Malta led to Germany's *Führer* Adolf Hitler coming to the aid of his Italian ally. Previously, Italian efforts to subjugate Malta had involved bombing raids against strategic targets: namely the airfields and Grand Harbour. But the RAF together with AA gunners had been more than capable in countering Italian air attacks.

On 11 January 1941, Adolf Hitler issued Directive No. 22 resulting in the deployment of German forces to Albania and Libya in support of Italian efforts. X.Fliegerkorps was despatched to Sicily with the main task of attacking British naval forces and disrupting lines of communication between the western and eastern Mediterranean. In addition, Luftwaffe units would operate from airfields in Libya, striking at British port facilities and bases in the region.

In the first few months of 1941, Malta had to contend with a far more determined enemy intent on neutralizing the island's defences. But instead of maintaining the pressure, Hitler turned his attention to other fronts and the Luftwaffe on Sicily was redeployed accordingly. The Luftwaffe did not return until later in the year. On 2 December 1941, Hitler's Directive No. 38 outlined the transfer of Luftwaffe units to Sicily and North Africa under the command of Feldmarschall Albert Kesselring, who was tasked with ensuring air supremacy, to seize control of the Mediterranean between southern Italy and North Africa and, especially, with subjugating Malta.

The aim of Kesselring's air offensive against Malta was essentially to end its effectiveness as an Allied base. This involved targeting the island's airfields and wearing down the fighter defence and striking at Grand Harbour and its Dockyard facilities, as well as the Royal Navy's submarine base at nearby Lazzaretto. When Malta was sufficiently weakened, it was intended that the island be seized by a powerful Italo-German force involving paratroopers and amphibious landings.

Malta's air war would vary in intensity. This is due in part to seasonal changes but also depended largely on Axis commitments. On the Eastern Front, especially, air operations

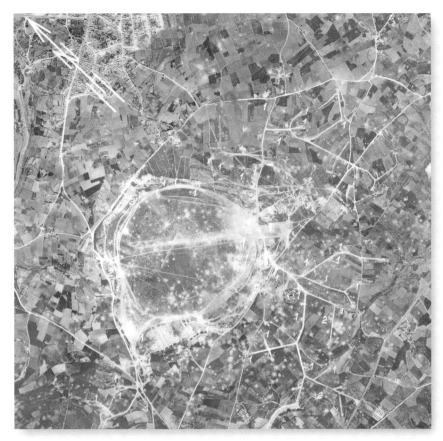

Ta' Qali (Ta Kali), situated in central Malta, was a former civil airport that was commandeered as a fighter base. This photograph was taken from a Ju 88 of 1.Aufklärungsgruppe/122 at 13:47 hrs on 20 April 1942, following the arrival at Malta of 47 Spitfires from the American carrier USS *Wasp*. Number 601 (County of London) Squadron would be based at Luqa, and 603 (City of Edinburgh) Squadron at Ta' Qali. Spitfires, widely dispersed in and around the airfield, are indicated by the number 1; four wrecked machines are shown as 2. Although at least 45 seemingly serviceable aircraft can be seen, four are almost certainly scrapped 'decoys' left outside unfinished underground hangars in an effort to mislead the Luftwaffe. What look like four low-flying aircraft are visible beyond the airfield perimeter.

Grand Harbour was another important Axis target. Malta Dockyard remained in operation throughout the siege. In this undated press photograph, a 4-inch gun is being replaced on a warship. This is French Creek, looking towards Senglea.

were dictated by the weather, with severe winter conditions restricting flying. Aircraft were transferred from one front to another, as and when the situation dictated. This affected Axis air strength on Sicily, where a reduced Luftwaffe presence meant that the Regia Aeronautica had to contend with Malta. In comparison to German raids, those carried out by Italians were noticeably less determined and achieved limited results. During such periods, Malta was able to recover and reorganise. This fundamental flaw in Axis strategy, together with the failure to proceed with an invasion of the island, contributed to the eventual outcome of the battle.

For the British, the priority was to ensure a situation where Malta could hold out against Axis air attacks and at the same time continue offensive operations. Malta-based bombers could easily reach military and industrial targets in Sicily and Italy. These were important, but it was the war in North Africa that mattered. Both sides engaged in the Desert Campaign were reliant on reinforcements and a steady resupply of fuel, military vehicles, heavy weapons and ammunition. Italo-German forces had little option but to rely on sea routes between Italy and ports in Libya and Egypt, with Malta and its striking forces in-between. As well as having Malta, Britain was further advantaged in retaining control of Egypt and the Suez Canal, in possessing Gibraltar and in being able to rely on a powerful Mediterranean Fleet.

RAF and Axis airfields

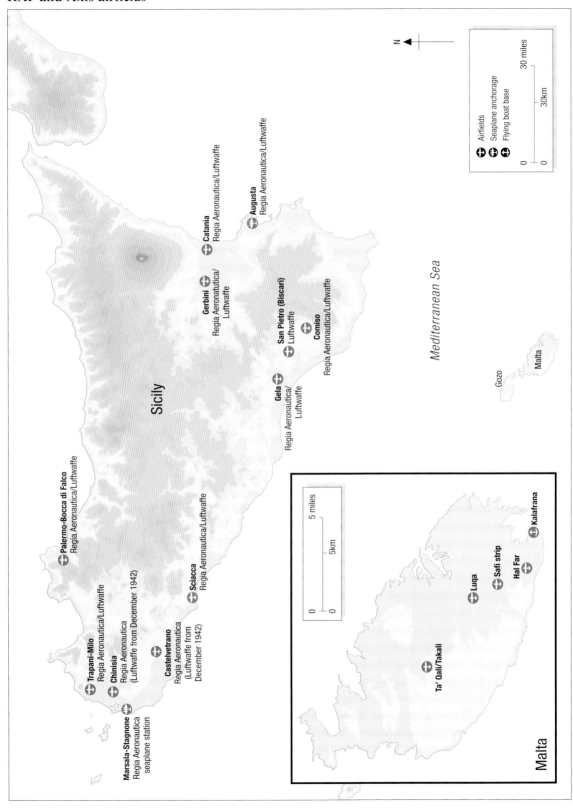

Catania
Regia Aeronautica/Luftwaffe

Augusta
Regia Aeronautica/Luftwaffe

Gerbini
Regia Aeronautica/
Luftwaffe

San Pietro (Biscari)
Luftwaffe

Comiso
Regia Aeronautica/Luftwaffe

Gela
Regia Aeronautica/
Luftwaffe

Mediterranean Sea

Gozo

Malta

Sicily

Palermo–Bocca di Falco
Regia Aeronautica/Luftwaffe

Sciacca
Regia Aeronautica/Luftwaffe

Trapani-Milo
Regia Aeronautica/Luftwaffe

Chinisia
Regia Aeronautica
(Luftwaffe from December 1942)

Castelvetrano
Regia Aeronautica
(Luftwaffe from
December 1942)

Marsala-Stagnone
Regia Aeronautica
seaplane station

Ta' Qali/Takali

Luqa

Safi strip

Hal Far

Kalafrana

Malta

Airfields
Seaplane anchorage
Flying boat base

30 miles

30km

0

0

5 miles

5km

0

0

THE BATTLE

START OF THE AIR WAR

In May 1940, the C-in-C, Mediterranean, at the request of the AOC, Mediterranean, had agreed to the loan of four Sea Gladiators, then in storage at Kalafrana. Six RAF pilots, none of whom had previous fighter experience, were hastily trained and, on 4 June 1940, a fighter flight was formed at Hal Far. On the outbreak of war, a continuous stand-by of two Gladiators was maintained during daylight hours (those still in storage provided a ready source of spare parts). This small improvised unit won the admiration of all, although, and probably because it was rare to ever see four in the air, the perception was such that there were only three such aircraft. It is not known who christened the machines 'Faith', 'Hope' and 'Charity', or even when. Neither is it certain which, if any, were actually referred to by name. But an enduring myth had been created.

The Battle of Malta began shortly before 07:00hrs on 11 June 1940, when air raid sirens warned of an imminent attack. Ground observers noted that two air formations, each of five Italian S.79s, approached at 12,000 to 14,000 feet before dropping bombs in the vicinity of Hal Far and the Dockyard area. During the next 40 minutes, successive waves carried out further attacks. Aircraft were engaged by AA guns and intercepted by Gladiators, albeit with little effect. At Fort St Elmo, six ORs of the Royal Malta Artillery lost their lives and at nearby French Creek one OR of the Royal Artillery was killed. There would be several air raid warnings but no further bombing raids until that evening. Grand Harbour was the main target, but bombs also fell elsewhere, including at Verdala barracks, resulting in injuries to 15 infantrymen. AA guns were again in action as were, according to some reports, Malta's Gladiators. Coastal guns also opened fire on what were thought to be enemy motor torpedo boats off Grand Harbour. What were, in fact, three Royal Navy small craft, were all sunk; at least four Maltese naval ratings died. There would be little material damage during the day, but in addition to military casualties, at least 16 civilians lost their lives and many more were injured. Raids continued on an almost daily basis for the rest of the month.

Malta's Gladiators withstood 2ª Squadra Aerea until the end of June. By that time, the RAF and Fleet Air Arm (FAA) had been provided with additional aircraft. With the fall of France expected imminently, two naval Swordfish training squadrons, then in French North Africa, were re-tasked. A dozen or

Initially, Malta had only Italian raids to contend with. In 1940, the standard bomber was the Savoia-Marchetti S.79 'Sparviero', such as this machine of 258ª Squadriglia, 109º Gruppo, 36º Stormo B.T., operating out of Castelvetrano, Sicily. Italian bomber crews were known for operating at high-level, achieving little in the process. These early raids did little to weaken the resolve of the Maltese.

so were flown to Gibraltar. A similar number went to Malta, where they would operate as 830 Squadron, thus providing a limited anti-shipping striking force. Even more welcome was the acquisition on 21 and 22 June of five Hurricanes. These had been destined for North Africa but were retained at Malta by permission of the AOC-in-C, Middle East. They arrived just in time, for on the 21st, two Gladiators had been written off in landing accidents (one aircraft was subsequently rebuilt from the wrecks). One of two American-built Lockheed Hudsons, which had led the Hurricanes during their flight from Britain, was also retained and put to use as a long-range reconnaissance machine.

On the 22nd, the RAF achieved its first air victory when Gladiators were scrambled to intercept an S.79. Flight Lieutenant George Burges in Gladiator N5519 carried out a successful stern attack. The Italian machine, with both engines on fire, fell in the sea off south-east Malta. There were two survivors, both of whom became prisoners of war. The next day, Burges, again flying N5519, accounted for an MC.200. This, too, crashed offshore, the pilot baling out and being taken prisoner. The first success by a Hurricane pilot is thought to have occurred on 3 July, when an S.79 was brought down off the coast. The Hurricane was attacked by an Italian fighter when landing and crashed as a result. The pilot was unhurt, but his aircraft was a write-off.

On Tuesday morning, 16 July, Flight Lieutenant Peter Keeble was scrambled together with Pilot Officer Allan McAdam, the former in a Hurricane and the latter in a Gladiator. At 09:11hrs, the pair was informed about approaching bombers and fighters. Keeble acknowledged. Before long, those monitoring events heard machine-gun fire. Keeble's Hurricane was then seen, trailing smoke and diving with a CR.42 close behind. The two fighters crashed close together near Marsaskala. Peter Keeble was the first RAF fighter pilot to lose his life in the defence of Malta. Machine-gunners of 1st Battalion The Dorsetshire Regiment claimed to have brought down the CR.42. The pilot, tenente Mario Benedetti, who had somehow survived the crash, died of his injuries in hospital.

On the last day of July, a CR.42 and a Gladiator were shot down. The Italian pilot, capitano Antonio Chiodi, died. Flight Lieutenant Peter Hartley baled out. He was rescued from just offshore, badly burned, but would survive. His would be the only Gladiator lost in combat.

FIRST NAVAL SURFACE ENGAGEMENTS

The evacuation from Malta of some civilians (mainly British naval officers' families) had begun shortly before Italy's entry into the war. A further operation was postponed in late June 1940, after Royal Navy warships tasked with escorting merchant ships east from Malta clashed with Italian destroyers transporting an anti-tank unit to Libya. Submarines had already accounted for several ships in the Mediterranean, but this would be the first surface engagement between the region's naval powers. The Italian Regia Marina destroyer *Espero* was sunk with heavy loss of life. The British cruiser HMS *Liverpool* sustained minor damage. An anti-submarine operation by destroyers and aircraft resulted in four successes within three days. *Console Generale Liuzzi* was scuttled after being depth-charged and forced to the surface; the commander stayed on board after the order to abandon ship. They became prisoners of war, as did the crew from *Uebi Scebeli*. There were no known survivors from *Argonauta* and nearly all perished on *Rubino*.

The delayed operation took place some days later, commencing on 7 July. It was centred around two convoys ('M.F.1' and 'M.S.1') with Fleet stores and evacuees from Malta destined for Alexandria.

At the same time, the Italians were intending to escort from Naples to Tripoli a convoy comprising five merchant ships with tanks and other war materiel. Events would lead to another clash at sea and the first encounter with Italian aircraft employed in an anti-shipping role. No ships were lost during the action off Calabria, but the cruiser HMS *Gloucester* was damaged by a bomb, resulting in 27 casualties. Before the operation was over, Swordfish from the carrier *Eagle* carried out an attack on Augusta, sinking RN *Leone Pancaldo*; most of her crew were saved. (The Italian destroyer was later raised, put back into service and sunk for a second time in 1943.) Continuing Italian air attacks failed to prevent 'M.F.1' from reaching Alexandria on 13 July. 'M.S.1' followed two days later.

OPERATION 'HURRY'

Battle casualties, flying accidents and mechanical problems combined to reduce further Malta's remaining Gladiators and Hurricanes. An effective defence needed a steady reinforcement of fighters. The solution was to ferry Hurricanes by aircraft carrier to within flying range of the island.

On 23 July 1940, the aircraft carrier *Argus* left Greenock in Scotland with 12 Hurricane Mk I fighters and 14 RAF pilots comprising 418 Flight. *Argus* reached Gibraltar a few days later and on the 31st proceeded east in company with the carrier *Ark Royal* and warships of Vice Admiral James F. Somerville's Force H. Diversionary operations were to be conducted at both ends of the Mediterranean, with those in the east undertaken by Admiral Sir Andrew B. Cunningham's Alexandria-based Mediterranean Fleet.

The passage of Force H was not without incident: an attack by Italian bombers in the evening of 1 August resulted in the shooting down of at

August 1940, Operation 'Hurry': Hurricanes on the flight deck of HMS *Argus* soon to take off for Malta.

least one S.79 by Skuas from *Ark Royal*. Among those killed was bomber brigade commander, generale Stefano Cagna. That night, *Ark Royal* was detached with other ships for an additional task. In the early hours of the 2nd, Swordfish from the carrier were despatched to Sardinia, the objectives: Elmas (Cagliari) airfield and the nearby port. In the event, the crew of one Swordfish were killed in a take-off accident and another crew were taken prisoner when they force-landed after being damaged by AA fire. In a separate action, carrier-borne fighters engaged Italian flying boats shadowing the fleet, shooting down one and severely damaging another.

Meanwhile, the appropriately codenamed Operation 'Hurry' saw the Malta-bound Hurricanes taking off from the flight deck of *Argus* to cover the final 380 miles (611.5km) to their destination. The aircraft were divided into two groups of six, each led by a Skua flown by 418 Flight pilots. Two Sunderlands from Gibraltar transported ground crew personnel and spare parts (with more on the way by submarine). Luqa was reached two hours and 20 minutes later. One Hurricane was written off and a Skua was damaged when landing. All other aircraft landed without mishap. To their surprise, the ferry pilots, who had expected to return to the UK, now learned that they were to join the fighter flight. Soon afterwards, this became 261 Squadron.

In September, three American-built Glenn Martin 167s (Marylands) arrived for a new reconnaissance unit: 431 Flight (re-titled 69 Squadron in January 1941), while the pre-war 3 Anti-Aircraft Cooperation Unit, from which several of the original Gladiator pilots had been drawn, was disbanded.

In the first days following Italy's declaration of war, Malta's fighter force consisted of no more than four operational Sea Gladiators. This Gladiator is shown at Luqa in late summer or autumn of 1940. The pilot is Sergeant Harry W. Ayre, who had arrived during Operation 'Hurry'.

RAF statistics for the first four months of hostilities are revealing. Of a total of 161 air raid alerts, 76 were false alarms. The remainder heralded 36 day and 13 night bombing raids, 21 reconnaissance missions and 15 fighter patrols. There had been more than 50 alerts in June. In October, there were just ten.[2]

MALTA CONVOYS

Malta was to be kept supplied through a series of complex naval operations. These were undertaken with merchant ships and escorting warships of the Mediterranean Fleet (from Alexandria) and Force H (from Gibraltar). Operations also provided for unloaded vessels at Malta to depart under escort. The first Malta convoy was coordinated with a move to send reinforcements via Gibraltar for the Mediterranean Fleet (Operation 'Hats'). These were the new armoured carrier *Illustrious*, battleship *Valiant* and the anti-aircraft cruisers *Coventry* and *Calcutta* (Force F). The carrier *Ark Royal*, cruisers *Renown* and *Sheffield* together with destroyers (Force B) would provide support as far as the central Mediterranean. Submarines were to be deployed on a patrol line between Sicily and Libya and, in an effort to reduce enemy air attacks, RAF aircraft of 202 Group would attack enemy airfields in Libya.

Prior to commencing operations, four destroyers were sent from Alexandria via Malta to reinforce Force H at Gibraltar. Off Cape Bon, on 23 August, HMS *Hostile* struck a mine and had to be sunk by friendly forces. *Nubian* was beset by a mechanical problem, necessitating a return to Malta, accompanied by *Hero* and *Mohawk*. The destroyers, having been joined by a fourth, *Janus*, reached Gibraltar a few days later.

Events got underway in the evening of Thursday, 29 August when convoy 'M.F.2' comprising the Royal Fleet Auxiliary *Plumleaf*, refrigerated

2   Statistics vary slightly depending on source.

At Luqa airfield in the summer of 1940, fighter pilots of the recently formed 261 Squadron wait at dispersal, a modified Malta bus. Sergeant Oswald R. 'Drac' Bowerman (left) plays chess with Sergeant Dennis K. Ashton. In the background is Sergeant Eric N. Kelsey.

Soon, Malta's Gladiators were joined by a few Hurricanes. This machine, seen landing at Luqa, was one of the first to be sent to Malta.

cargo ship *Cornwall* and freighter *Volo* left Alexandria covered by four destroyers. These were followed, in the early hours of the 30th, by HMS *Warspite* (with Admiral Cunningham), a second battleship, *Malaya*, the fleet carrier *Eagle*, and cruisers *Orion* and HMAS *Sydney*, screened by nine destroyers. Third Cruiser Squadron (Vice Admiral John C. Tovey, second-in-command of the Mediterranean Fleet) provided additional fire power with HM Ships *Kent*, *Gloucester* and *Liverpool* and a screen of three destroyers. That morning, Force B also left Gibraltar with Force F.

Cunningham's force was sighted by Italian air reconnaissance within hours of leaving port. The first enemy contact for the east-bound group occurred the next day (31st), when Skuas from *Ark Royal* intercepted and shot down a Cant Z.506B, followed, a few hours later, by a Cant Z.501. Another Cant was claimed following an attack by Gladiators from *Eagle*.

Soon, the merchant ships came under air attack. *Cornwall* was hit aft and badly damaged, but still able to continue. At day's end, another threat loomed when air reconnaissance reported Italian warships about 140 miles (225km) to the north-west, steering towards the convoy. But by mid-afternoon on 1 September, the Italian fleet had reversed course back towards Taranto.

Meanwhile, several related operations were set in motion. Earlier, two destroyers of Force H had been detached to the north of the Balearics in order to transmit spurious signals (Operation 'Squawk'), the intention being to mislead enemy forces and at the same time detract from another task. This commenced in the early hours of 1 September, when nine Swordfish from *Ark Royal* bombed Elmas airfield, near Cagliari (Operation 'Smash'). That same night, Forces B and F parted, the former turning south-east towards Malta and the latter returning to Gibraltar. On the 2nd, *Ark Royal* again flew off nine Swordfish for another attack on Cagliari airfield and a power station (Operation 'Grab'), but with unsatisfactory results due to less than ideal weather conditions.

Plumleaf and *Volo* reached Malta that morning. *Cornwall* was not far behind. HM Ships *Valiant*, *Coventry* and *Calcutta* landed additional stores before re-joining the fleet and setting course eastward.

During the day, Italian-crewed Ju 87s – so-called *Picchiatelli* – were used for the first time against the Mediterranean Fleet, dive bombing warships off Malta, albeit without result. (*Picchiatelli* would commence operations against Malta two days later.)

While passing through the southern Aegean on 4 September, Swordfish from *Eagle* and *Illustrious* struck at targets on Rhodes. At dawn, *Orion* and *Sydney* (7th Cruiser Squadron) accompanied by the destroyers *Ilex* and *Decoy* bombarded the island of Scarpanto/Karpathos. Several Italian 'E-Boats' were encountered, one of which, *MAS 537*, was sunk by HMS *Ilex*. After enduring further bombing attack, the first warships re-entered Alexandria Port on Wednesday night.

In the period 31 August to 4 September, as many as 14 Italian aircraft were probably destroyed in the air and on the ground and at least six FAA machines had been written off, including four that failed to return from attacking Rhodes. Malta's one and only reconnaissance Hudson was also lost after it was mistakenly attacked by naval Fulmars and forced-landed in Tunisia.

At the end of September, HM Ships *Liverpool* and *Gloucester* reached Malta with stores and personnel ('M.B.5'). 'M.B.6', with a three-fold purpose, followed in October. This operation was designed to bring to Malta four merchant ships from Alexandria ('M.F.3') and to cover the departure of convoys at Malta and Greece. It would also involve an attack by carrier-borne aircraft of strategic targets on the Aegean island of Leros. On 8 October the Mediterranean Fleet departed Alexandria, followed that night by the Malta-bound convoy. For the next two days, enemy submarines shadowed the force, albeit without result. But on the 11th, the destroyer HMS *Imperial* was severely damaged by a mine south of Malta. The merchant ships arrived at Malta that afternoon. In the early hours of the following morning (12th) HMS *Ajax* encountered Italian *torpedinieri* (torpedo boats, similar to the British destroyer) some 80 miles (129km) south-east of Sicily. During a fierce exchange of fire *Ajax* took seven direct hits, resulting in numerous casualties and impairing the ship's fighting efficiency. Even so, the cruiser succeeded in sinking the Italian *Airone* and *Ariel*, and severely damaging *Artigliere* (subsequently sunk by the cruiser *York*).

Later that day, S.79s carried out high-level bombing attacks, resulting in shockwave damage to the carrier *Eagle*. Carrier-borne fighters and AA fire accounted for three bombers; others returned to base damaged and with dead or wounded aircrew. During the night of 13/14 October, Swordfish from *Illustrious* attacked Leros, all returning safely to the carrier. Before 'M.B.6' was concluded, the Royal Navy suffered one more casualty, when the cruiser *Liverpool* was struck by an aerial torpedo and had to be taken in tow to Alexandria. She would be out of service for a year.

At the end of October, Wellington bombers were flown from Britain to be based temporarily at Luqa, before continuing to the Middle East. The following month, Wellingtons of 37 Squadron arrived, staying briefly before flying to Egypt. The initial detachment remained, however, and in December was given a new identity as 148 Squadron.

In 1940, Luqa, then primarily a bomber base, catered for aircraft in transit. As the airfield was constructed in an area of quarries and small fields with low stone walls, landings and take-offs could be hazardous. This Wellington is believed to have been transporting Major General Bernard C. Freyberg and Lieutenant-Colonel Keith L. Stewart from the UK to the Middle East, when it crashed on landing on 23 September 1940.

A low-flying 261 Squadron Hurricane heads south over Dwejra Lines, just to the north-west of Ta' Qali.

Another naval operation in November was 'M.B.8.'. This multi-faceted and extremely complex undertaking included the delivery of supplies to Greece ('A.N.6'), transfer of vessels from Greece to Port Said ('A.S.5') and five Malta-bound merchant ships ('M.W.3') with general stores, fuel and cased petrol; in addition, the Malta Minesweeping Flotilla would be reinforced by HMS *Abingdon*. Four cargo vessels at Malta were to depart under escort for Alexandria ('M.E.3'), while the monitor *Terror* was to sail for Suda, Crete, accompanied by the Australian destroyer *Vendetta*. Another element of 'M.B.8' was Operation 'Coat', during which the battleship *Barham*, cruisers *Berwick* and *Glasgow* and four destroyers would join the Mediterranean Fleet and at the same time bring to Malta stores and troops (including 4th Battalion The Buffs). Before 'M.B.8' was over, Swordfish from the carrier *Illustrious* also struck at Cagliari (Operation 'Crack'). This was followed two nights later (11/12 November) by a successful raid on Italian shipping at Taranto in conjunction with a combined cruiser and destroyer force (Operation 'Juggernaut').

On 17 November, HMS *Argus* despatched to Malta 12 Hurricanes accompanied by two FAA Skuas (Operation 'White'). In the event, eight RAF fighters ran out of fuel en route and the crew of a Skua became prisoners of war after mistakenly flying to Sicily, where they were shot down by AA. There were three more supply runs before the end of the month: RAF reinforcements from Britain disembarked from the cruiser *Newcastle* on the 19th, to be followed one week later by four cargo ships ('M.W.4') and, on the 28th, by two more with guns and military stores (Operation 'Collar'). In mid-December, seven cargo ships left Alexandria and Port Said in two sections ('M.W.5A' and 'M.W.5B'), before merging and continuing towards Malta, arriving safely on the 20th. As was the established procedure, vessels awaiting departure left under escort. On this occasion, four went to Alexandria and two sailed for Gibraltar. During the latter task, an escorting destroyer, *Hyperion*, was severely damaged by a mine and subsequently torpedoed by an accompanying warship. Most of the crew survived.

By this time, Allied successes in Egypt and Libya had led to the greater part of the Italian army still in Cyrenaica to withdraw within the defences of Bardia, which surrendered in early January 1941. Tobruk followed. Italian efforts in Greece were also foundering. As 1940 drew to a close, Germany came to the aid of its ally, units of the German X.Fliegerkorps transferring from Norway to Sicily. By mid-January 1941, Luftwaffe front-line aircraft numbered some 80 Ju 87 dive-bombers, 80 Ju 88 bombers, 12 long-range reconnaissance Ju 88s, Heinkel He 111 bombers and 34 Messerschmitt Bf 110 twin-engine fighters. These would be joined in coming weeks by additional aircraft including, in February, Bf 109 fighters.

OPERATION 'EXCESS' AND THE 'ILLUSTRIOUS BLITZ'

The first convoy of 1941 was codenamed 'Excess' and was part of a series of operations with the main aim of resupplying British forces on Malta and on the Greek Front. At the same time, vessels already at Malta would depart under the protection of escorting warships in two convoys ('M.E.5½' and 'M.E.6').

On Monday, 6 January, the cruisers *Gloucester* and *Southampton* (Force B) embarked at Suda Bay, Crete, more than 500 army and RAF personnel for transport to Malta, leaving with the destroyers *Ilex* and *Janus*. That afternoon, the cruiser HMS *Bonaventure* and four destroyers left Gibraltar with four merchantmen recently arrived from Britain. These were *Essex*, destined for Malta, and three Greece-bound vessels, *Empire Song*, *Clan Cumming*, and *Clan Macdonald*. A fourth, *Northern Prince*, had been driven ashore during a storm and was unable to continue. Initially, the convoy steered a deception course westward before changing direction and under cover of darkness re-entering the Mediterranean, there to meet warships of Vice Admiral Somerville's Force H. This included the carrier *Ark Royal*, battlecruiser *Renown*, battleship *Malaya* and cruiser *Sheffield*.

At the other end of the Mediterranean, the cruisers *Orion* and *York* left Alexandria in the early hours of the 7th. They were to cover the oiler RFA *Brambleleaf* while she was escorted by corvettes of Force C through the Kasos Strait, before joining the cruisers HMS *Ajax* and HMAS *Perth* and covering the westward passage of the corvettes.

Two hours later, Force A sailed with Admiral Cunningham's flagship *Valiant* and another battleship, *Warspite*, together with the carrier *Illustrious* and seven destroyers. During the afternoon, the commissioned auxiliary supply ship *Breconshire* and steamship *Clan Macaulay* ('M.W.5½') also left Alexandria, bound for Malta with the cruiser *Calcutta* and destroyers *Diamond* and *Defender*.

Force B arrived at Malta from the Aegean early on Wednesday (8th). After disembarking troops and refuelling, three of the four warships left to rendezvous with Force H (HMS *Janus* would join the fleet screen on completion of pre-planned repairs); the Australian cruiser *Sydney* and destroyer flotilla leader HMAS *Stuart* sailed to join Force A. Also en route from Suda at this time were the corvettes of Force C and *Orion*, *York*, *Ajax* and *Perth* of Force D. After joining Cunningham next morning (9th), *Sydney* and *Stuart* were detached to Alexandria in connection with another task, while Force D parted company to provide convoy cover and AA support for 'M.E.6' the following day (10th).

Further west, five Swordfish had been flown off *Ark Royal* early on the 9th to join 830 Squadron on Malta. Force H met Force B a few hours later. The first enemy air assault followed that afternoon. During a high-level bombing attack, *Malaya* and *Gloucester* were near missed but escaped being damaged. Two S.79s were shot down. Having accomplished his task, Somerville parted company with *Bonaventure* and that evening Force H set course for Gibraltar.

The next encounter was on Friday morning (10th). Four British warships and two Italian torpedo boats clashed, resulted in superficial damage to *Bonaventure*. The Italian torpedo boat *Vega* was engaged at close range before being torpedoed by *Hereward*, blowing up with the loss of nearly all on board. Less than half-an-hour later, HMS *Gallant* detonated a mine, the explosion blowing away the bow and resulting in numerous casualties. The destroyer, still somehow afloat, was taken in tow to Malta.

By this time, 'M.W.5½' had arrived and 'M.E.6' had left port, to be followed later that morning by 'M.E.5½'. Cunningham, having made the rendezvous with 'Excess' south-south-east of Pantelleria, was now within range of enemy aircraft on Sicily. At 12:35hrs, and a few minutes after an unsuccessful torpedo attack by two S.79s, there appeared two formations of German-crewed Ju 87s. In an assault lasting just six and a half minutes the carrier was struck by six bombs, rendering the flight deck unusable, destroying aircraft and putting guns out of action. Additional damage resulted from three very near misses.

Aircraft still airborne from *Illustrious* were ordered to land at Malta. (One Swordfish and a Fulmar failed to arrive; all except the Fulmar's air gunner were rescued.) After refuelling, the Fulmars returned to cover *Illustrious* and at least six Ju 87s were claimed destroyed during a dive-bombing attack that afternoon. *Illustrious* succeeded in reaching Grand Harbour that night and was berthed at Parlatorio Wharf.

Essex had also arrived at Grand Harbour, bringing 24 HAA guns, 18 LAA guns, 12 searchlights, 300 tons of naval stores (including 54 depth charges), 12 Hurricanes, 3,300 tons of ammunition, 20 submarine torpedoes, 24 warheads and 2,600 tons of seed potatoes. The cost so far had been HMS *Gallant* and *Illustrious* severely damaged, the former with 80 casualties, including 65 dead, and the latter with more than 200 killed, injured and missing, including RAF personnel in transit. (A continuation of planned offensive actions would not take place due in part to damage to *Illustrious*.)

On 11 January warships escorting the six slow merchantmen from Malta to Egypt were attacked by Ju 87s, now operating at extreme range. Of about 180 casualties from *Gloucester* and *Southampton*, half were dead or would die of their injuries. *Southampton* could not be saved and was later torpedoed and sunk by the cruiser *Orion*. (A Walrus seaplane, which was airborne after having been launched from *Gloucester*, could not be recovered and was written off; the crew were picked up.)

At Parlatorio Wharf in Malta's Grand Harbour, a massive effort was underway to enable the departure of HMS *Illustrious*. The destruction resulting from precision dive-bombing attacks had transformed the carrier into a mass of torn and twisted steel. Five Swordfish and four Fulmars had been written off. As the dead and wounded were brought ashore, fires were extinguished and dockyard workers began making hasty repairs.

The remaining merchantmen of 'Excess' arrived at Piraeus on the 12th. There, the cruisers HMS *Orion* and HMAS *Perth* transhipped for onward passage to Malta more than 600 mainly army personnel. They arrived without mishap on the 14th.

The aircraft carrier HMS *Illustrious* (visible under the floating crane at centre) under attack at Grand Harbour in mid-January 1941.

Italian and German aircrew with a Macchi C.200 of 1° Stormo caccia terrestre (probably 88ª Squadriglia, 6° Gruppo), at Catania, in Sicily, in early 1941. Until the arrival in Sicily of the Luftwaffe, this was the only Italian fighter that could compare with the Hurricane in combat. (Bundesarchiv, Bild 101I-423-0163-16)

With the exception of a raid on 13 January, during which HMS *Illustrious* escaped being hit, the enemy initially made little effort to finish off the carrier. In the meantime, between 12 and 16 January, Malta-based Wellingtons conducted night-time bombing raids in an attempt to destroy enemy aircraft on the ground at Catania. Two crew members died when their Wellington was damaged by *Flak* and had to ditch; another crew were lost when their aircraft was shot down. (A prisoner of war would state during interrogation that at Catania nine aircraft had been written off and another was seriously damaged.)

For those on Malta, the lull continued until 16 January, when, soon after 14:00hrs, German bombers struck, further damaging *Illustrious* and causing widespread destruction in the harbour area. *Essex* was hit amidships and set on fire, and *Perth* sustained damaged below the waterline aft (she left for Alexandria that night). Malta's defenders, having learned from previous raids by Italian dive-bombers, responded with an anti-aircraft 'box barrage' and this no doubt contributed to upsetting the aim of Stuka pilots. Axis aircrews also had to contend with fighters, including 806 Squadron Fulmars, operating from Ħal Far.

The Germans returned two days later, this time concentrating on Luqa and Ħal Far. But they failed to put the airfields out of action for long, nor was Malta's fighter defence rendered ineffective. On the contrary, some Hurricane pilots flew three or four sorties on the 18th and the following day, when there was a final concerted effort to sink *Illustrious*. There was a series of attacks, the first heavy raid occurring shortly after 09:35hrs and lasting 43 minutes. The next major attack commenced at 12:47hrs. *Illustrious* was further damaged, this time by near-misses on the port side. The all clear sounded at 13:30hrs. Additional material damage on this date included the minesweepers *Decoy* and *Beryl*.

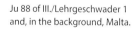

Ju 88 of III./Lehrgeschwader 1 and, in the background, Malta.

On completion of a successful mission, *Ritterkreuzträger* Oberleutnant Gerhard Richter of III./Lehrgeschwader 1 is presented with flowers by the unit *'Spieß'*.

The Luftwaffe had provided a demonstration of what to expect for as long as the battle continued. As one Hurricane pilot remarked years later, 'until the advent of the Luftwaffe it would seem to have been a gentleman's air war'.

Operations for the period 16 to 19 January 1941 resulted in the loss of one FAA and one RAF fighter pilot and two Fulmars and a Hurricane. Three Swordfish, a Wellington and a Hurricane were written off on the ground. German fatalities amounted to at least 33 aircrew and ground personnel, including those who died as a result of Wellington bombers targeting Catania. In the air, four Ju 88s and four Ju 87s were destroyed. The Italians lost two pilots together with one MC.200 and a CR.42. A Cant. Z.506B air-sea rescue machine was also shot down. Other aircraft were written off on returning to Sicily, often as a result of emergency landings.

At sea, some 300 lives had been lost: Royal Navy, Royal Marines, embarked RAF personnel and merchant seamen. On Malta, of more than 60 fatalities, most were civilian victims of the first day of what became known as the '*Illustrious* Blitz', when the Dockyard and surrounding area had suffered widespread destruction.

HMS *Illustrious* was able to leave Malta during the night of the 23rd, arriving under her own power at Alexandria two days later. For the next few weeks, Fulmars of 806 Squadron stayed as much-needed reinforcements for Malta's air force. *Illustrious* later continued to the United States, where she would undergo months of repair before she again put to sea. At Malta, meanwhile, machine guns and 2-pdr pom-poms were removed from the battle-damaged *Essex* and *Gallant* and mounted on *Breconshire*. She would continue to supply Malta, both independently and during convoy operations, until her end 15 months later.

MESSERSCHMITT BF 109s JOIN BATTLE

By the end of January 1941, the RAF had on strength Hurricanes and Gladiators (261 Squadron), Short Sunderland flying boats (228 Squadron detachment), Marylands and a PRU Spitfire (69 Squadron, formerly 431 Flight) and Wellingtons (148 Squadron). There were two FAA units equipped with Fulmars (806 Squadron) and Swordfish (830 Squadron). At the end of the month, six more Hurricanes flew in from North Africa and additional fighter pilots arrived by Sunderland. With sufficient Hurricanes to hand, the Gladiators were now relegated for meteorological flights.

Malta played a small but nonetheless important role in February, when Luqa served as the jumping off point for the first ever British airborne operation, codename 'Colossus'. During the night of 10/11 February, some three-dozen officers and men were transported in converted Whitley bombers and parachuted into southern Italy. There, they attempted to destroy the Tragino Aqueduct, which provided water to the strategically important ports of Brindisi, Taranto and Bari. In this, they were partially successful. The aqueduct was damaged, but repairable; the saboteurs were captured and one, an Italian anti-fascist, later executed.

In the weeks following the 'Illustrious Blitz', some Luftwaffe units were redeployed to North Africa in support of Generalleutnant Erwin Rommel's recently arrived Deutsches Afrikakorps. The pressure on Malta was maintained, however, for in early February, Messerschmitt Bf 109 Es of 7./Jagdgeschwader 26 were transferred from Germany, south to Gela, Sicily. The outstanding performance of *Staffelkapitän*, Oberleutnant Joachim Müncheberg, had already resulted in 23 victories and earned him the coveted *Ritterkreuz* (Knight's

Infantrymen were employed in a variety of roles during the battle. This is defence post LQ8 at Luqa airfield in 1942, where a combined army and RAF team worked under Lieutenant Clifford Clark (3rd from left) of the Royal West Kents.

Cross). It was soon evident that the Hurricane was outclassed by the faster, cannon-armed Bf 109, especially when flown by experienced fighter pilots. During the next four months, 7./Jagdgeschwader 26 (joined briefly in March and May by Bf 109s of Jagdgeschwader 27) would dominate the skies over and around Malta, claiming at least 42 air victories, 20 of which were credited to Müncheberg (including one during the unit's brief involvement in the German invasion of Yugoslavia) and, incredibly, all without a single operational loss.

Müncheberg's Bf 109s appeared over Malta for the first time in the afternoon of 12 February, when they provided fighter escort for a bombing raid by several Ju 88s of III./Lehrgeschwader 1. Müncheberg brought down one Hurricane – his 24th victory – and Feldwebel Werner Leibing claimed two more. One Hurricane was damaged and force-landed at Luqa. Another was shot down, the pilot baling out. A third disappeared without trace: the flight commander, Flight Lieutenant Gerald Watson, had only recently transferred to fighters. But at this early

In February 1941, Bf 109 Es of 7./Jagdgeschwader 26 arrived at Gela, in Sicily. 7.Staffel commenced operations over Malta on 12 February, escorting bombers of III./Lehrgeschwader 1. This unique image is a record of that occasion.

stage of the war, it was standard procedure for the senior officer to lead, as opposed to a more experienced fighter pilot of lesser rank. Inflexibility was but one of the failures of the British military.

The Luftwaffe had the edge with regard to tactics, too. Hurricanes frequently had a problem in gaining sufficient height due to being scrambled too late. RAF fighter pilots were further disadvantaged by having to rely on outdated flying formations. The *Times of Malta*, published daily throughout the siege, did much to bolster spirits, informing the public of the (unintentionally inflated)

DIVE-BOMBING ATTACK ON GRAND HARBOUR (PP. 36–37)

On 23 March 1941, units of Sturzkampfgeschwader 1 carried out two attacks following the arrival at Grand Harbour of convoy 'M.W.6', comprising the merchantmen *City of Lincoln*, *City of Manchester*, *Clan Ferguson* and *Perthshire*, together with escorting warships. Here, a Ju 87 Stuka (**1**) levels out over Senglea (**2**). Two destroyers are anchored in Dockyard Creek (**3**). Smoke and dust are from bombing attacks on the cruiser HMS *Bonaventure* (**4**), moored at Hamilton Wharf in French Creek. During the second raid, some damage was caused to shipping (a stoker on board *Bonaventure* was killed and several ratings were wounded); one Hurricane was lost (the pilot baled out), and four Ju 87s failed to return (of a total of eight crewmen, just one survived).

toll inflicted on the enemy. The reality was often very different and it would be many months before the RAF on Malta learned to adapt.

There were five alerts on 26 February. Early in the morning, several Bf 109s escorted a Ju 88 over Malta. 'Raiders passed' sounded less than half an hour later. Nearly five hours passed before the next air raid warning. What followed was an attack reminiscent of those experienced during the '*Illustrious* Blitz'. It was an indication of what Malta could expect for as long as the Luftwaffe was in Sicily. Enemy aircraft were estimated to total 30 Ju 87s, 12 Ju 88s, ten Dornier 215s (probably Messerschmitt Bf110s), ten He 111s and 30 Bf 109 and Italian CR.42 fighters. Luqa airfield was severely damaged and at least six Wellingtons were destroyed on the ground. Three Hurricanes failed to return; another force-landed. The Luftwaffe lost four Ju 87s (one crew survived to become prisoners of war).

On 26 February 1941, Luqa airfield was targeted in a major bombing raid. The Stuka of Hauptmann Helmut Mahlke, *Gruppenkommandeur* of III./Sturzkampfgeschwader 1, returned to Comiso, Sicily, severely damaged by anti-aircraft fire and with 184 bullet holes following an encounter with a Hurricane. (Chris Goss)

On 22 March, 7./Jagdgeschwader 26 accounted for five Hurricanes and their pilots within just seven minutes. It was the latest in a series of one-sided engagements. However, the Hurricane had shown that it was quite capable of dealing with the more vulnerable Ju 87 Stuka. This was again demonstrated the very next day, following the arrival at Grand Harbour of all four merchantmen of convoy 'M.W.6'. Some 14 Hurricanes were scrambled in response to the second of two raids, involving approximately 30 Ju 87s and escorting fighters. One pilot baled out of his Hurricane when it was fired on and set ablaze – by the rear gunner of a Ju 87. But on this occasion, the Luftwaffe came off worse. The RAF and AA claimed between them at least 20 Ju 87s destroyed or damaged; in fact, four Ju 87s failed to return. Just one Stuka pilot survived.

This iconic image has been published many times since the Second World War. It has always been accepted that this was the Norwegian merchantman *Talabot*, soon after reaching Malta on 23 March 1942. In fact, this is a Cameron-class ship, almost certainly *Perthshire*. She also arrived at Grand Harbour on 23 March – but in 1941. Like *Talabot*, she was bombed while moored at the same location. *Perthshire* was damaged but not severely and sailed from Malta on 19 April 1941, reaching Alexandria three days later.

In the eastern Mediterranean, the Royal Navy together with the Royal Australian Navy had achieved a major success off Cape Matapan in late March, sinking three Italian heavy cruisers and two destroyers and damaging a battleship and a destroyer. The following month, three Italian destroyers and five merchant ships en route to Tripoli were sunk or immobilized by the 14th Destroyer Flotilla but at the loss of the British *Mohawk* and more than 40 of the ship's company.

SPRING–SUMMER, 1941

Malta served as a transit point for aircraft of all types. Aircraft also came and went depending on operational requirements. In March, aircrew and ground staff of 148 Squadron departed for Egypt. Between April and the end of June, naval ferrying operations resulted in more than 200 Hurricanes being flown to Malta. Some remained as reinforcements and some flew on to join the RAF in the Western Desert.

There were now at Malta enough Hurricanes for a second fighter formation. On 1 May, C Flight, 261 Squadron was placed on readiness for the first time. Based at Hal Far, the nucleus of the new unit (soon retitled 185 Squadron) consisted of pilots and ground crews from 261 Squadron, with additional ground personnel from Egypt.

A day later, the first Beaufighters of 252 Squadron arrived from England and were soon providing air support for an east-bound convoy ('Tiger') for General Sir Archibald P. Wavell's forces in North Africa, which ended with four of five merchant ships reaching Alexandria. At the same time, a slow convoy with two tankers ('M.W.7B') departed Alexandria for Malta, followed the next morning, 6 May, by a fast convoy ('M.W.7A') with four supply ships and *Breconshire*. All of the ships arrived safely.

Sergeant John K. 'Angus' Norwell in 261 Squadron's stand-by bus.

In mid-1941 the parity shifted between opposing air forces in the central Mediterranean. With the war in the desert progressing satisfactorily for Axis forces, the priority for Adolf Hitler in June would be the German invasion of the Soviet Union (Operation 'Barbarossa'). Accordingly, German aircraft in Sicily and Libya were redeployed. Soon, 7./Jagdgeschwader 26 was re-tasked, flying south to Libya. As the Luftwaffe vacated its Sicily bases, they were replaced by Italian units. For a few months the RAF would once again have only the Regia Aeronautica to contend with.

Meanwhile, in England, 213, 229 and 249 (RAF) squadrons embarked for the Middle East. Ground personnel were transported in a separate convoy to pilots, who were ferried with their Hurricanes on board the carriers *Eagle*, *Furious* and *Ark Royal*. When within flying distance of Malta, they were be guided by Fulmars of the recently-formed 800X Squadron (FAA), following which, the latter were to continue to Crete. Four Beaufighters of 252 Squadron, now at the end of their Malta detachment, would take over for the leg to Egypt.

Before the carriers reached Gibraltar, the commanding officer of 800X Squadron was ordered to exchange his new

Fulmar IIs with *Ark Royal*'s old Fulmar Is. This benefited the carrier's fighter wing, but put at risk the task allocated to 800X Squadron. In the event, two Fulmars were beset by mechanical problems and the pilots were forced to ditch. One crew, including the squadron commander, was interned in Vichy North Africa; the other crew was rescued. Of the three RAF squadrons, two would end up in Egypt, less one Hurricane that crashed en route (the pilot survived as a prisoner of

war). However, after landing at Malta, the pilots of 249 Squadron were dismayed to learn that they were to remain so that 261 Squadron could be relieved. The latter unit then took over 249's Hurricanes and departed with them for the Middle East. 249 Squadron was thus redeployed, with battle-worn Hurricanes and unfamiliar, albeit experienced, Malta ground crews transferred from 261 Squadron. The invasion of Crete by German airborne forces also resulted in 800X Squadron remaining on Malta.

In November 1940, 261 Squadron relocated from Luqa to RAF Station Ta Kali. These RAF personnel are shown shortly afterwards, in early 1941. The pristine condition of the Hurricane is indicative of a recent arrival.

Number 249 Squadron had a well-deserved reputation following its performance in the Battle of Britain and this was, perhaps, reflected in the attitude of the new arrivals, more than half of them officers ('too much class distinction', according to one airman). Furthermore, the same airman observed, when the air raid warning sounded, some seemed disdainful of old Malta hands who were quick to take cover. This would soon change. On 25 May, 7./Jagdgeschwader 26 bid farewell with a final low-level strafe of Ta' Qali. The Bf 109s struck as 249 Squadron pilots sat strapped in the cockpits of their fighters, awaiting the order to scramble. Within seconds, two aircraft were on fire, three more were damaged and two pilots and a number of ground personnel had been injured.

June 1941 began with Air Commodore Hugh Lloyd taking over from Air Vice-Marshal Forster Maynard, Malta's AOC since the start of

Ju 87s of Sturzkampfgeschwader 1 attract AA fire as they cross Malta after a bombing raid in early 1941. (Bundesarchiv, Bild 101I-422-0045-27A)

hostilities. Among reinforcements that month were fighter pilots of 46 Squadron, like 249, another unit that had participated in the Battle of Britain. Subsequently, these pilots were re-organized as 126 Squadron, joining 249 at Ta' Qali. At about the same time, the RAF's striking force welcomed the return of a detachment of 148 Squadron Wellingtons from Egypt. Later the following month, 12 Hurricane Mk IIs were allocated for another new formation: the Malta Night Fighter Unit (MNFU).

ITALIAN SEABORNE ATTACK ON GRAND HARBOUR

Having been tasked once again with subjugating Malta, the Italians proceeded with an audacious plan whereby Xª Flottiglia MAS of the Regia Marina would mount a simultaneous strike at a recently arrived convoy ('Substance') and the submarine base at neighbouring Marsamxett Harbour. Following a number of reconnaissance missions and two aborted starts, the operation got underway. The attacking force comprised two motor torpedo boats (*motoscafo anti sommergibili – MAS*), *451* and *452*, and the sloop *Diana*, the latter transporting nine one-man explosive motor boats (*motoscafo di turismo – MT*) and a two-man motor torpedo boat (*motoscafo da turismo silurante – MTS*). *Diana* also towed a motor boat (*motoscafo da turismo lento – MTL*) carrying a pair of two-man 'human torpedoes' (*siluro a lenta corsa – SLC*) each with a detachable explosive bow. In overall command was capitano Vittorio Moccagatta on board *MAS 452*.

The force left Augusta in the early evening of 25 July. The plan is described in detail on pages 44–45. While events were taking place, the Regia Aeronautica was to carry out two diversionary attacks (in the event, there were two air raid warnings, at 02:53 and 04:13hrs). Back-up plans took into account various eventualities.

Unfortunately for the Italians, they were detected by RDF at 20:55hrs. Motor boats were audible to those on Malta's north-east cast from 22:20hrs onwards. By 23:00hrs the force had approached to within 14 miles (22.5km) of the island. All guns were manned and the air raid warning sounded. It was assumed that the target had to be a departing convoy, but no ships were due to leave. St Elmo light was therefore switched on for five minutes in an effort to lure the enemy. A Swordfish striking force was despatched, only to return to base without having sighted anything. At about 04:45hrs the all clear sounded. One minute later, a small craft was seen fast approaching St Elmo. An explosion followed: one of the *MT*s had detonated

Naval convoys were the lifeblood of Malta. In July 1941, Operation 'Substance' delivered to Malta supplies and personnel. On the 23rd, the cruiser HMS *Manchester* and the destroyer HMS *Fearless* were severely damaged during Italian aerial attacks. *Manchester* was able to withdraw to Gibraltar. *Fearless* had to be sunk to avoid capture. This view of the burning vessel is from the merchantman *Port Chalmers*.

at the harbour entrance, the blast bringing down one span of the breakwater viaduct steel bridge, effectively blocking the entrance. The pilot, sottotenente Aristide Carabelli, was killed. The blast may also have caused the deaths of maggiore Teseo Tesei and secondo capo Alcide Pedretti, who had crewed one *SLC*. Defence Electric Lights (DELs) now came on. For several minutes the illuminated area off the harbour entrance was criss-crossed by tracer rounds as every available close-range weapon commenced firing.

At dawn, movement was observed offshore, prompting a further bout of firing. Two targets were blown up. By this time, Hurricanes had been scrambled, the pilots strafing whatever they saw. In the words of Vice Admiral, Malta, this final action 'turned a failure into a disaster'.

Fifteen Italians had been killed, including the commander, Moccagatta. Eighteen were captured (among them Costa and Barla). Italian fighters intervened at daybreak. Two were lost (only one pilot survived). A Hurricane was also shot down. The pilot baled out into the sea, not far from a stationary *MAS 452*. He clambered on board, finding only dead Italians, and awaited rescue. The vessel was later towed into Grand Harbour. The second *MAS* was sunk.

In July 1941, the Italian Navy's La Decima Flottiglia MAS conducted an operation against the British submarine base at Marsamxett Harbour and the newly arrived 'Substance' convoy in neighbouring Grand Harbour. In the event, the only damage was to the mole bridge of the breakwater at the entrance of Grand Harbour. One of the vessels, *MAS 452*, was subsequently recovered, seen here, while moored at Fort St Angelo.

AUTUMN, 1941

Italian aerial activity decreased significantly during August and September. RAF Headquarters recorded 24 and 29 alerts respectively, down from 69 in July. Italian efforts to destabilize Malta were having little effect and Allied convoys were still getting through, but at a cost in shipping, aircraft and lives. Operation 'Substance' in July resulted in all six merchantmen reaching Malta. One, *Sydney Star*, was damaged in an Italian torpedo boat attack. Italian air attacks resulted in further damage to the cruiser *Manchester* and destroyer *Firedrake*. The former was put out of action for nine months and the latter for six months. Another destroyer, *Fearless*, was immobilized by an aerial torpedo and had to be sunk by friendly forces.

Operation 'Halberd' in September resulted in HMS *Breconshire* and six of seven merchantmen arriving. *Imperial Star* was torpedoed and abandoned after efforts were made to scuttle her (she later sank). The battleship *Nelson* was also torpedoed and put out of commission for six months.

'Substance' and 'Halberd' delivered tens of thousands of tons of stores, including foodstuff, ammunition, AA guns, spare parts for military ordnance and equipment, together with some 4,500 reinforcements, among them, 4 Heavy Anti Aircraft Regiment Royal Artillery, 32 Light Anti Aircraft Regiment Royal Artillery and 11th Battalion The Lancashire Fusiliers.

ITALIAN SEABORNE ATTACK ON GRAND HARBOUR, 26 JULY 1941

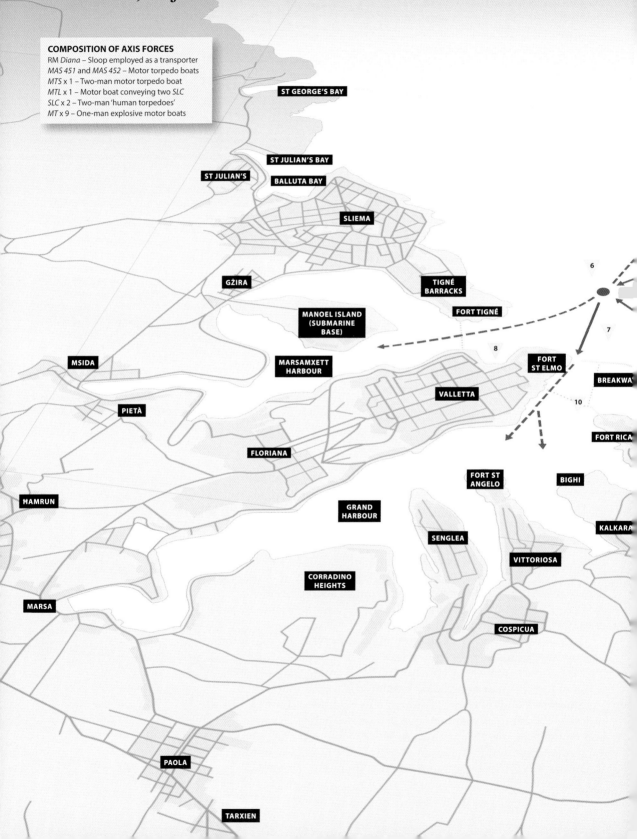

COMPOSITION OF AXIS FORCES
RM *Diana* – Sloop employed as a transporter
MAS 451 and *MAS 452* – Motor torpedo boats
MTS x 1 – Two-man motor torpedo boat
MTL x 1 – Motor boat conveying two *SLC*
SLC x 2 – Two-man 'human torpedoes'
MT x 9 – One-man explosive motor boats

ST GEORGE'S BAY

ST JULIAN'S BAY

ST JULIAN'S

BALLUTA BAY

SLIEMA

GŻIRA

TIGNÉ BARRACKS

FORT TIGNÉ

6

MANOEL ISLAND (SUBMARINE BASE)

7

MSIDA

MARSAMXETT HARBOUR

8

FORT ST ELMO

VALLETTA

BREAKWA

PIETÀ

10

FORT RICA

FLORIANA

FORT ST ANGELO

BIGHI

ĦAMRUN

GRAND HARBOUR

KALKARA

SENGLEA

VITTORIOSA

MARSA

CORRADINO HEIGHTS

COSPICUA

PAOLA

TARXIEN

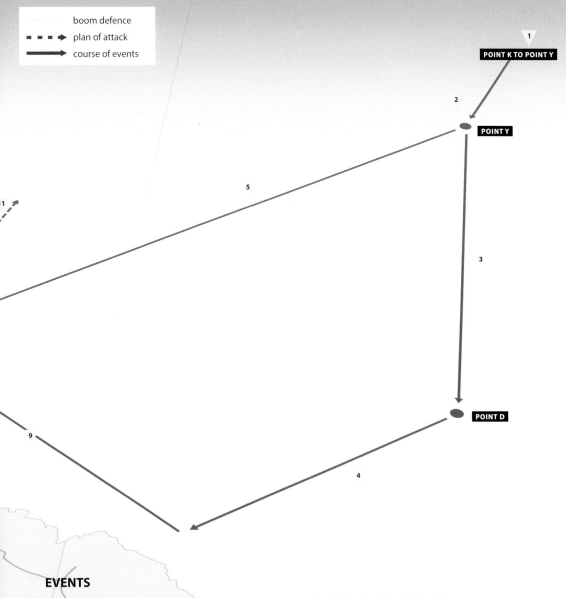

1

POINT K TO POINT Y

2

POINT Y

5

3

11

POINT D

9

4

EVENTS

Plan of attack

(This included detailed contingency arrangements.)

In company with *MAS 451* and *MAS 452*, RM *Diana* towing one *MTL* and, with nine *MT* and one *MTS* hoisted, departs Augusta at 18:15hrs on 25 July 1941. All proceed to position 36° 00′ N, 14° 35′ E (Point K – 7.6 miles/12.2km north-north-east of Fort St Elmo) to arrive by 23:00hrs.

Events

1. At Point K, all stop and *Diana* disembarks the *MT* and *MTS* and slips the *MTL*. *Diana* retires northwards and stands by to assist the *MAS* if necessary.

2. From Point K, both *MAS* (one with the *MTL* on a short tow), followed by the *MTS* and nine *MT* proceed to position 044°, 3.5 miles/5.6km, St. Elmo Point (Point Y), to arrive at 01:34hrs. All stop and the *MTL* is released from tow.

3. From Point Y, the *MTS* and *MT* continue south with the *MAS* to Point D.

4. At Point D, the *MTS* and *MT* alter course to 229° towards Point M at Dragut Shoal.

5. The *MTL* (with both *SLC* on board), in the meantime, proceeds from Point Y to Point M (to be joined there by the *MTS* and *MT*).

6. 02:37hrs: The *MTL* launches both *SLC*.

7. Maggiore Teseo Tesei and secondo capo Alcide Pedretti take one *SLC* to the anti-submarine net at St. Elmo breakwater, and there set a timed charge (to detonate at about 04:30hrs) before returning to the *MTL* and then re-joining the *MAS*.

8. After avoiding harbour obstructions, tenente Franco Costa with sergente Luigi Barla in the second *SLC* attack submarines at Lazzaretto, again using a timed charge (set to detonate at 05:16hrs), before withdrawing for pick-up by the *MTS*.

9. Meanwhile, the *MTS* and *MT* approach, parallel to shore, to Point M.

10. As soon as the first *SLC* charge detonates, the *MT* are to follow the *MTS* through the breached breakwater net and towards designated targets in Grand Harbour (passing through an opening between the boom and the coast). Both *MAS* are to wait to recover personnel on conclusion of their mission.

Withdrawal

11. On completion of the mission the two *MAS* were to meet the *MTL*, which by this time was to have picked up the first *SLC* crew, transship all personnel and take in tow the *MTL*. The *MAS* would then be joined by the *MTS*, which was to have recovered the second *SLC* crew and pilots of the *MT*. The force would then return to Sicily.

boom defence

plan of attack

course of events

ŻABBAR

Luftwaffe aircrews had a healthy respect for Malta's anti-aircraft capabilities and gun sites were frequently singled out for attention. Here, bombs explode not far from a heavy AA gun battery.

A further 1,000+ all-ranks, mainly 8th Battalion The King's Own Loyal Regiment, arrived on warships from Gibraltar on 2 August.

Operation 'Status II' resulted in another Hurricane delivery in mid-September. Later that month, offensive air operations over Sicily were extended when some Hurricanes were converted into 'Hurri-bombers' with Light Series bomb racks capable of carrying 40-lb (18kg) general-purpose and 25-lb (11 kg) incendiary bombs.

Malta's submarine force had been designated the Tenth Submarine Flotilla at the start of September. Striking forces experienced further changes and developments the following month. Wellingtons of 104 and 40 squadrons flew in from Britain, while those of 38 Squadron departed to Egypt. In the early hours of 18 October, *Ark Royal* flew off 828 (FAA) Squadron, which was to be based at Hal Far. All 11 Albacores reached Malta, together with one Swordfish (one was lost en route). Three days later, the Royal Navy's Force K (cruisers *Aurora* and *Penelope* and destroyers *Lance* and *Lively*) moved to Grand Harbour.

Preventing Axis supplies from reaching Libya remained a priority. The harassment and disruption of enemy communications also continued. In October, air attacks were carried out on targets in Sicily, southern Italy, Sardinia and Libya. Marylands and PRU Spitfires covered Italian convoy routes and there were shipping strikes by Wellingtons, Blenheims and Swordfish torpedo bombers of 830 Squadron. Presumably as a result of Allied successes, on the 18th, Axis convoys to Tripoli were temporarily suspended. When operations resumed, they would result in one of the most successful Allied naval engagements to date.

DESTRUCTION OF THE '*MAESTRALE*' CONVOY

For Malta, 8 November began with a brief incursion in the morning by a pair of Macchis. There followed an ineffectual bombing raid towards midday, when two MC.202s were lost, including one in a collision with a Hurricane. Only the Hurricane pilot survived. Raids continued after dark, but, again, with negligible result. Malta-based Wellingtons and Albacores were busy in the meantime, bombing targets in Italy and Sicily. Off Cape Spartivento, Sardinia, Blenheims also struck at a small convoy, leaving one vessel on fire, but losing two aircraft in the process. Further east, however, the Royal Navy would achieve an important victory.

Throughout the war, the Germans relied on Enigma, an ingenious encryption device, to send and receive secret messages. But Enigma had been compromised very early on. Transmissions were intercepted and passed to specialists at Bletchley Park in Buckinghamshire, England, where they were decrypted and translated. In the early afternoon of 7 November, a brief signal mentioned a convoy '*Maestrale*' (so named after the leading Italian escort destroyer). A few hours later, there was a follow-up message referring to 'the important convoy proceeding to Tripoli'.

Referred to by various names, including the prosaic *51. Seatransport*, this was an important convoy destined for Libya with 78 men and supplies: 4,359 tons of military stores and 217 vehicles. It comprised five German and Italian cargo ships (*Duisburg*, *Maria*, *Rina Corrado*, *Sagitta* and *San Marco*) and two Italian tankers (*Conte di Misurata* and *Minatitlan*). Italian destroyers were in attendance, while several more destroyers and the cruisers *Trento* and *Trieste* provided distant cover. After sailing from Naples, the convoy had taken a circuitous route so as to give Malta a wide berth and at the same time avoid detection. But reconnaissance flights by 69 Squadron were already monitoring shipping in the Ionian Sea and by the 8th, the convoy had been located. That afternoon, Force K was despatched from Malta to intercept. In a brief, largely one-sided, engagement, shortly after midnight, Force K accounted for all five merchantmen and both tankers – nearly 40,000 tons of shipping – as well as the destroyer *Fulmine*. A second destroyer, *Libaccio*, was subsequently claimed by the British submarine *Upholder* (*P 37*).

EARLY U-BOAT OPERATIONS

After an initial and largely uneventful foray into the Mediterranean in 1939, German submarines (*Unterseeboote*, or U-boats) resumed activities in September 1941 with 23.Unterseebootsflottille operating out of Salamis, in the Saronic Gulf. In December, 29.Unterseebootsflottille was established, based initially at La Spezia, northern Italy. (The latter flotilla would absorb boats of the former in May 1942.) U-boats in the Mediterranean begun to take toll of Allied lives and shipping in October 1941, going on to achieve three successes the following month.

On 12 November, 34 Hurricanes of 242 and 605 squadrons took off from the carriers *Argus* and *Ark Royal*, initial destination: Malta. Number 258 Squadron, awaiting onward passage at Gibraltar, was expected to follow. All three units were to have continued to the Western Desert. But this was not to be. While returning to Gibraltar the next day, *Ark Royal* was torpedoed by *U.81*, sinking 14 hours later. All but one of the crew survived what was, both for the Royal Navy and for Malta, a tremendous blow. Personnel still at Gibraltar were diverted elsewhere. Pilots and aircraft of 242 and 605 squadrons would stay at Malta. Before the end of the month, the battleship *Barham* was torpedoed by *U.331* and blew up. Well over 800 lost their lives. Two days later, on 27 November, at least 138 perished when the Australian sloop *Parramatta* was torpedoed off Tobruk by *U.559*.

November also saw the first U-boat losses in the Western Mediterranean. *U.433* was depth charged by the corvette HMS *Marigold* on the 16th (there were 38 survivors). *U.95* was torpedoed by the Dutch submarine *O 21* less than two weeks later (12 of the crew were rescued).

In November, the number of Axis vessels sunk in the Mediterranean far exceeded those of the Allies, although, when taking into account *Ark Royal* and *Barham* (together they weighed well over 50,000 tons), there was little difference in terms of tonnage.

Successes by Malta-based aircraft and warships included the sinking by Force K of the Italian transport *Adriatico*, tanker *Iridio Mantovani* and the

A 1942 photograph of British and Maltese servicemen in the underground Coastal Defence operations room, part of War Headquarters at Lascaris, Valletta.

Italian destroyer *Alvise da Mosto* between 30 November and 1 December. At the start of December, it was ordered that 'the most important' Axis reinforcements were to be transported to North Africa mainly by air.

At sea, both sides were suffering. December would be especially grim for the Mediterranean Fleet and particularly Force K (recently strengthened by additional warships). On the 14th, *U.557* torpedoed the Royal Navy cruiser *Galatea*, with a loss of well over 400 lives. On the 18th, an attack at Alexandria by Italian 'human torpedoes' severely damaged the battleships *Queen Elizabeth* and *Valiant*, the destroyer *Jervis* and tanker *Sagona*. A day later, an Italian-laid minefield claimed four warships from Malta. The cruiser *Neptune* was lost with 763 all-hands; there was one survivor. Another 73 perished when the destroyer *Kandahar* was mined (she was later torpedoed and sunk by HMS *Jaguar*) and HM Ships *Aurora* and *Penelope*, were damaged. By the end of December, more Axis tonnage had been lost in comparison to Allied vessels, although there was little difference numerically.

Notwithstanding their undoubted effectiveness, U-boats alone were not going to achieve naval superiority in the Mediterranean. So far, the Regia Marina had failed to safeguard Axis convoy routes between Italy and North Africa, while Italian air power had been unable to neutralize or even weaken Malta's defences. It was abundantly clear to the German high command that without further Luftwaffe involvement, Malta would remain an effective Allied base and, for as long as this continued, Axis supply lines between Europe and North Africa would be under constant threat.

RETURN OF THE LUFTWAFFE

Towards the end of November 1941, a combined German and Italian command and staff element for the Mediterranean was created, with Generalfeldmarschall Albert Kesselring, commanding Luftflotte 2 in Russia,

MALTA GARRISON, JANUARY 1942

Headquarters
HQ Malta Command
Armoured Corps
No. 1 Independent Troop, Royal Tank Regiment (Malta Tanks w.e.f. 27 January 1942)
Artillery
HQ RA
Command Fixed Defences Malta
12 Field Regiment (Signal Section and Light Aid Detachment.)
HQ 26 Defence Regiment RA
      15/40 Defence Battery RA
      48/71 Defence Battery RA
      13 Malta Defence Battery
HQ 4 Coast Regiment RA
      6 Coast Regiment RA
      10 Coast Battery RA
      23 Coast Battery RA
HQ 1 Coast Regiment RMA
      1 Coast Battery RMA
      2 Coast Battery RMA
      3 Coast Battery RMA
      4 Coast Battery RMA

      'Z' Battery RA
HQ 7 LAA [Light Anti-Aircraft] Brigade RA
HQ 74 LAA Regiment RA
      59 LAA Battery RA
      182 LAA Battery RA
      225 LAA Battery RA
HQ 32 LAA Regiment RA
      55 LAA Battery RA
      98 LAA Battery RA
      223 LAA Battery RA
HQ 4 Searchlight Regiment RA
      484 Searchlight Battery RA
      8 Searchlight Battery RMA
HQ 3 LAA Regiment RMA
      30 LAA Battery RA (TA)
      22 LAA Battery RA
      10 LAA Battery RA
HQ 65 LAA Regiment RA
      194 LAA Battery RA
      196 LAA Battery RA

      15 LAA Battery (Relief)
HQ 10 HAA [Heavy Anti-Aircraft] Brigade RA
12 AA Gun Operations Room (Class A)
HQ 4 HAA Regiment RA
      5 HAA Battery RA
      6 HAA Battery RA
      186 LAA Battery RA
HQ 7 HAA Regiment RA
      10 HAA Battery RA
      13 HAA Battery RA
      27 HAA Battery RA
HQ 10 HAA Regiment RA
      190 HAA Battery RA

      191 HAA Battery RA
      222 HAA Battery RA
HQ 2 HAA Regiment RMA
      6 HAA Battery RMA
      7 HAA Battery RMA
      9 HAA Battery RMA
HQ 11 HAA Regiment RMA (T)
      20 HAA Battery RMA (T)
      21 HAA Battery RMA (T)
      23 HAA Battery RMA (T)

      14 HAA Battery (Relief)
Engineers
Works Services Malta
HQ Fortress RE Malta
16 Fortress Company RE
24 Fortress Company RE
      173 Tunnelling Company RE
      127 Bomb Disposal Section
      128 Bomb Disposal Section
      1 Works Company RE
      2 Works Company RE
RE Malta Section
Signals
Malta Signal Company
Special Wireless Section
Infantry
HQ Northern Infantry Brigade
      4th Battalion The Buffs
      8th Battalion The Manchester Regiment
      2nd Battalion The Royal Irish Fusiliers
      1st Battalion The King's Own Malta Regiment (Less 26 Drivers I.C. and with modified transport)
      2nd Battalion The King's Own Malta Regiment
HQ Central Infantry Brigade
      1st Battalion The Durham Light Infantry (arrived 27 January 1942)
      11th Battalion The Lancashire Fusiliers
      1st Battalion The Cheshire Regiment
      2nd Battalion The Queen's Own Royal West Kent Regiment
HQ Southern Infantry Brigade
      2nd Battalion The Devonshire Regiment
      8th Battalion The King's Own Loyal Regiment
      1st Battalion The Hampshire Regiment
      1st Battalion The Dorsetshire Regiment
      3rd Battalion The King's Own Malta Regiment

In May 1942, 4 (Western) Infantry Brigade was established with 4 Buffs, 8 King's Own and 1 DLI.

Static Defence Group King's Own Malta Regiment (later 10 Battalion KOMR)
Malta Independent Company
Malta Volunteer Defence Force
Supply and Transport
Supply, Transport and Barrack Services, Malta

32 Company Royal Army Service Corps
Medical
Royal Army Medical Corps Malta
90 General Hospital (To be formed from existing sources)
45 General Hospital (Skeleton)
39 General Hospital (To be formed from drafts sent in convoy W.S.11-X)
57 Field Hygiene Section
161 Field Ambulance
15 Field Ambulance
Convalescent Depot
Army Dental Corps
Ordnance
Depot and Workshop Royal Army Ordnance Corps Malta
4 Mobile Laundry
Provost
H.P.S.C. Detention Barracks, Malta

Prisoner of War Camp (for 1,500–2,000 prisoners, to be formed only when required)
HQ 226 Company Corps of Military Police
    Six sections Corps of Military Police
Intelligence
Field Security Section
Pay
Pay Services Malta
Miscellaneous
Recruit Training Depot, Malta (under command Fixed Defences)
Records Office (Maltese Units)
Records Office (Maltese Auxiliaries)
Special Duties Staff, Malta
Officer Cadet Training Unit Malta
Command School
Command Gymnasium and Physical Training School, Malta
Rest Camp, Malta
Army Educational Corps, Malta

designated Commander-in-Chief South, subordinate to Mussolini, whose directions would be delivered through Italy's *Comando Supremo*. With the onset of winter and deteriorating flying conditions on the Eastern Front, the Germans began to transfer aircraft, south to Sicily. Other units were redeployed from Western Europe. On 2 December, Adolf Hitler issued Directive No. 38. Acting under the orders of Mussolini and in cooperation with Axis land and air forces in North Africa, Kesselring was tasked with achieving air supremacy in the central Mediterranean, subjugating Malta and thereby securing lines of communication between southern Italy and North Africa. Allied shipping was also to be targeted in order to cut off Allied supplies to beleaguered Malta and Tobruk, in Libya. Accordingly, Generalleutnant Bruno Loerzer's II.Fliegerkorps took over from the Regia Aeronautica during daylight operations over Malta.

The impact was quickly felt. The number of air raid warnings had risen to 52 in October and 87 the following month. In December, the RAF on Malta recorded 159 alerts. German raids, which began on a relatively small scale, increased in intensity towards the end of the month. Night-time nuisance raids by single bombers became routine. By day, bomber sorties were heavily escorted by the latest Messerschmitt Bf 109 F. It was the beginning of the end of the Hurricane's short-lived reign over Malta. On 22 December, the Luftwaffe recorded for the first time more than 200 sorties flown against Malta.

By mid-January 1942, an increasing number of German aircraft was arriving at Sicilian airfields. They included Bf 109s of Jagdgeschwader 53 (soon to be joined by II./Jagdgeschwader 3), Ju 88s (I. and 4./Nachtjagdgeschwader 2, Küstenfliegergruppe 606, Stab and I./Kampfgruppe 54, Kampfgruppe 806, Stab, II. and III. Kampfgruppe 77) and Bf 110s (III./Zerstörergeschwader 26).

The Regia Aeronautica under generale Silvio Scaroni in Sicily comprised 54° Stormo C.T. with MC.200s (16° Gruppo) and Re 2000s (377ª Squadriglia autonomo C.T.); further fighters (7° Gruppo) were detached at Pantelleria. In addition, there were S.79 bombers of 10° Stormo B.T. (30° and 32° Gruppi), Fiat CR.25 reconnaissance machines (173ª Squadriglia autonomo R.S.T.) and, at Pantelleria, S.79 torpedo bombers (278ª Squadriglia autonomo A.S.), as well as maritime reconnaissance, observation and sea rescue units.

There were also close to 200 aircraft on Sardinia, although these would not play a direct role in the renewed assault on Malta. The Axis order of battle remained fluid, changing as units of the Italian and German air forces were transferred to and from Sicily.

In recent months, Malta had strengthened and improved both defensive and offensive capabilities, not least by reinforcing the island garrison, increasing the number of heavy weapons and building up food, ammunition and fuel reserves. Three airfields were operational. In mid-January 1942, Luqa provided a base mainly for twin-engine types: Special Duties Wellington Flight, reconnaissance aircraft of 69 Squadron, Wellington bombers of 40 Squadron and Blenheims of 21 Squadron (the recent arrival of which allowed Blenheims of tour-expired 18 and 107 squadrons to depart). Two Hurricane squadrons, 126 and 249, were stationed at Ta' Qali. Hurricanes of 1435 Flight and 185, 242 and 605 squadrons were at Ħal Far, together with 828 and 830 (FAA) squadrons: the former equipped with Albacores and the latter with Swordfish. At the nearby seaplane base at Kalafrana, there was even a special operations Heinkel He 115 with spurious Luftwaffe markings (it was destroyed in a strafing attack in February 1942). Malta was now equipped with five Air Ministry Experimental Stations: AMES 241, 242, 501, 502 and 504. Heavy and light AA gun batteries were positioned all around the island. True, the Mediterranean Fleet and Force K in particular had incurred losses. However, the Tenth Submarine Flotilla was still a potent force. How the situation would develop in the face of recent losses and the possibility of further intensified attacks by the Luftwaffe remained to be seen.

The last alert of 1941 sounded at 23:45hrs on 31 December, heralding the new year with bombing raids on Ta' Qali and Luqa. Soon after 02:00hrs on 1 January 1942, Luqa was again targeted, a solitary bomber carrying out the first of eight attacks on this date.

The Luftwaffe now struck whenever the winter weather allowed, targeting airfields in particular. On Saturday morning, 3 January, three Ju 88s took off on a routine bombing mission from Catania. One pilot turned back when a

During the first few months of 1942, Malta's only available fighter continued to be the Hurricane. This is Z4941 of 185 Squadron landing at Ħal Far.

A low-flying Messerschmitt Bf 109 during a strafing attack at Hal Far.

parachute was accidentally deployed inside his aircraft. The remaining two bombers continued, escorted by an estimated 50 fighters. Twenty-two Hurricanes were airborne and waiting. AA also engaged, accounting for the first Bf 109 to be shot down over Malta. The pilot, Unteroffizier Werner Mirschinka, was killed. There was another event of note when a Ju 88, singled out by AA and several Hurricanes, was severely damaged. Deciding against ditching, the pilot, Oberleutnant Viktor Schnez, remained at the controls, allowing his crew to escape, before abandoning the aircraft himself. All four were taken prisoner. There would be occasions when survivors from a shot-down enemy bomber were rescued from the sea. However, this would be the one and only time when an entire crew survived after parachuting on to Malta.

Early January saw two changes of command. On New Year's Day, the Royal Navy's senior officer on Malta, Vice Admiral Sir Ralph Leatham, took over from Vice Admiral W. T. R. Ford. On the 5th, Major-General D. M. W. Beak arrived, allowing Major-General S. J. P. Scobell and his family to depart by air a few days later.

The new GOC had been on Malta for just two weeks when his residence was hit by a 500kg bomb. It failed to explode, but split the house in two, leaving the General stranded on the top floor. The experience seems to have had little effect on Beak, for two days later, he continued with a shake-up of the established routine, lecturing officers in the importance of and the need for improvement in leadership, endurance, discipline and 'The Offensive Spirit'. Physical training and cross-country runs, he informed them, would be instituted for all ranks under 40 years of age.

Malta's 'Poor Bloody Infantry' – the PBI – were the unsung heroes of the siege. They were required to toil at airfields in all kinds of weather, filling in bomb craters and assisting the air force in everyday tasks, from refuelling aircraft to preparing protective pens for aircraft and service vehicles. Such pens were laboriously constructed with rubble and using stone and earth-filled petrol cans. The PBI were needed to help unload stores whenever a convoy arrived and also took their turn in manning defence and beach posts in their respective battalion area. Even in time of war, the PBI engaged in manoeuvres and training exercises. Atrocious weather conditions failed to prevent Axis aircrews from mounting a series of attacks on 13 January. Neither did it stop an army inter-platoon 'march and shoot' competition (it was won by 2nd Battalion The Royal Irish Fusiliers). The impressions of those obliged to take part can only be imagined.

As well as encouraging what were perceived by the officer class as morale boosting tasks for the men, Beak also brought about a number of policy changes, the chief of which was the concentration of mobile reserves throughout the island and the adoption of an offensive role, as opposed to static defence, for those manning various posts.

RUBBLE WALL CAMOUFLAGE HELMETS

British Forces on Malta adopted a distinctive and unique camouflage scheme for vehicles, as well as equipment, from anti-aircraft guns to steel helmets. By late July 1941, helmets worn by military and civil personnel had been transformed with what was dubbed 'Malta wall' or 'rubble wall' camouflage. As they had been hand-painted, no two helmets were alike, but all adhered to a broadly similar style, with a yellow or sand-coloured base over which a pattern of darker brush strokes was applied (these might be grey, green or brown) to create a 'rubble' appearance, thus breaking up the helmet outline. Frequently, a formation sign was painted on one or both sides of the helmet. For example, the Royal Irish Fusiliers had a dark green inverted isosceles triangle, apex down, apparently on one side only, while the Buffs are thought to have adopted a system whereby each company was identified with a scarlet square, diamond, circle, triangle or hexagon on both sides. There were numerous and varied formation signs/flashes. After the end of the siege of Malta, 'rubble wall' camouflage helmets began to appear in other theatres. This can be explained by the redeployment of Malta-based units. For example, 1st Battalion The Dorsetshire Regiment, 2nd Battalion The Devonshire Regiment and 1st Battalion The Hampshire Regiment fought in Sicily and Italy as 231 Infantry Brigade before being withdrawn to take part in the Normandy landings. 4th Battalion The Royal East Kent Regiment (The Buffs) together with 234 Infantry Brigade comprising 1st Battalion The Durham Light Infantry, 2nd Battalion The Royal Irish Fusiliers (Faughs) and 2nd Battalion The Queen's Own Royal West Kent Regiment were despatched to the Dodecanese Islands in the Aegean, only to be annihilated as fighting formations while defending Kos and Leros in autumn 1943.

A fine example of a 'rubble wall' camouflage helmet, this one of 24 Fortress Company Royal Engineers. (Stephen Petroni)

On 22 January a Hurricane pilot finally succeeded in destroying a Bf 109 over Malta. But RAF fighter pilots were still being outperformed by their adversaries in the Luftwaffe. Three days later, five Hurricanes were shot down by Bf 109s (one pilot was killed) and two more were damaged.

In January, Operation 'M.F.2' (not to be confused with the 1940 operation of the same codename) saw the safe delivery of stores on board the commissioned infantry assault ship *Glengyle*. Operation 'M.F.3' (comprising convoys 'M.W.8A' and 'M.W.8B') followed. During this operation, an escorting destroyer, HMS *Gurkha*, was torpedoed by *U.133* on the 17th; most of the ship's company were saved. Three of four merchant ships, *Ajax*, *City of Calcutta* and *Clan Ferguson*, entered Grand Harbour on the 19th. 'M.F.3' brought 65 Light Anti-Aircraft Regiment Royal Artillery as well as a tank squadron for Malta's modest armoured force. A fourth transport, the Norwegian *Thermopylae*, had to divert with engine trouble to Benghazi. She was damaged in an air attack and subsequently sunk by friendly forces. Three of the ship's crew and 32 army reinforcements for Malta perished; three more died of their injuries. Among military stores lost were six Cruiser tanks. 'M.F.4' eight days later (27th) saw the return of *Breconshire* and arrival of the majority of three companies of 1st Battalion The Durham Light Infantry (1 DLI); another company was transported on an accompanying destroyer (the balance would arrive from Egypt by sea over the next few weeks).

Axis forces had also succeeded in transporting by sea reinforcements and supplies for Rommel's forces. There were losses, including the Italian liner

Just north-west of Grand Harbour and overlooked by Valletta is Manoel Island, where Lazzaretto served as a submarine base and as such was another important target during air attacks.

and wartime transport *Victoria*, sunk on the 23rd after being attacked by torpedo bombers from Malta. Some 350 lives were lost.

Towards the end of the month, Kesselring issued orders for a further intensification of attacks, to begin in early February, in order to eliminate Malta as an air and naval base. Wintry conditions were a hinderance for the RAF on Malta, with the unsurfaced airfields at Ħal Far and Ta' Qali prone to flooding. Furthermore, cover from view afforded by rain and cloud benefited the Luftwaffe. When the German assault began, attacks were directed mainly at airfields, the submarine base at Lazzaretto and neighbouring Grand Harbour. Residential areas also suffered, probably as a result of bomber pilots manoeuvring to avoid AA fire.

Both sides could be equally uncompromising in what had become an increasingly bitterly fought war. *HSL 129*, one of Malta's three air-sea rescue launches was strafed by Bf 109s on 4 February. Three men died and five were injured, including the skipper, who succumbed to his wounds a week later. More than one enemy rescue floatplane had also been targeted by Malta fighter pilots.

During the night of 11/12 February, the destroyer HMS *Maori* was bombed and sunk at her mooring in Grand Harbour. All but two of the crew, most of whom were ashore at the time, survived. Three nights later, the Italian steamer *Ariosto*, en route from Tripoli to Italy, was sunk with heavy loss of life, probably by *P 38* of the Tenth Submarine Flotilla. As a result

A destroyer at speed during the Second Battle of Sirte on 22 March 1942.

of Enigma intercepts, British intelligence was aware that *Ariosto* had been transporting Allied prisoners of war, but it is doubtful if this information was ever passed to Malta and, if it was, whether it could have been acted on in time. Just over a week later, *P 38* was lost with all hands.

Axis forces achieved a major success mid-month. Of three cargo ships of the latest Malta convoy ('M.W.9'), two were lost. The third was damaged and detached to Tobruk, later being escorted back to Alexandria.

On Malta, casualties were mounting at an alarming rate. There had been some 88 civilian fatalities in the first six months of hostilities, and nearly 300 in 1941. In January 1942, 85 civilians would lose their lives, many in the late afternoon/early evening of the 15th, and towards the end of an alert lasting more than 10½ hours. In Valletta, bombs fell at the Casino Maltese (an exclusive club), the Grandmaster's Palace and Regent Cinema. At the latter location, some 75 civilians and off-duty service personnel lost their lives and more than 60 were injured. Among the casualties were ratings who had escaped the recent sinking of their ship, *Maori*.

On the 27th, *Upholder* of the Tenth Submarine Flotilla sank the Italian steamer *Tembien*. Of about 625 on board, most were PoWs. According to an Enigma decrypt, only 78 were saved, together with 69 Italians and ten Germans.

Among those posted to Malta in February was Squadron Leader P. S. (Stan) Turner, who would take charge of 249 Squadron. He soon decided on some long overdue tactical changes. Malta's fighter pilots tended to use vic and line-astern formations, leaving themselves vulnerable to attack by German fighter pilots. The latter favoured a loose 'finger four' section, with aircraft positioned like the tips of fingers in an outstretched hand, or flew two aircraft in a wide-open line abreast formation, each pilot able to observe inwards towards his colleague and to cover the sky from 12 to six o'clock. It was due largely to Turner that the RAF on Malta now began to follow similar procedures.

Another decisive tactic implemented by Turner and Malta's outstanding operations controller, Group Captain A. B. 'Woody' Woodhall, would see

At Ħal Far, Wing Commander Hugh L. Dawson (right) waits out a raid with RAF and FAA officers.

OPPOSITE

A further three minefields (MT-25, MT-26 and MT-27) were established south of Malta in the first week of November 1942.

fighters scrambled in good time, to gain altitude south of the Island and well away from the approaching raid, thus achieving a height advantage for a fast diving attack.

During the night of 2/3 March, Palermo Harbour was targeted in two raids by Wellingtons of 37 Squadron. A steamship, *Cuma*, loaded with 1,314 tons of fuel and 1,790 tons of military supplies, was set on fire. On the 4th, *Cuma* blew up, the blast resulting in many casualties and causing widespread damage and destruction to shipping, buildings and port installations.

Number 37 Squadron had taken over from 40 Squadron, with aircraft, together with maintenance crews, flying in from Egypt. The detachment would pay a heavy price during its short stay at Luqa. As winter drew to a close and the Luftwaffe assault continued, the severity of attacks intensified. The Dockyard and airfields remained prime targets. By 20 March, 12 Wellingtons of 37 Squadron had been destroyed on the ground as a result of enemy action. Two more Wellingtons were written off in a take-off accident, which cost five aircrew their lives, while one of the maintenance party was fatally injured in an air raid. The squadron's one remaining serviceable aircraft returned to Egypt on 21 March.

SCHNELLBOOT OPERATIONS

Axis minefields off Malta resulted in more than 20 vessels being sunk or damaged. The Italian Navy began minelaying in early September 1940, when 112 mines were dispersed in two areas north-east of Grand Harbour and east-south-east of Delimara. There would be five such operations to April 1942, resulting in the placement of some 655 mines in eight locations north-east, south-east and south of Malta at distances ranging from nine to 27 miles (14.5 to 43.5km).

German minelaying started in early 1941, when magnetic and acoustic devices were dropped by aircraft, both offshore and in Grand Harbour. A more systematic procedure was adopted following the arrival in the Mediterranean of the first *Schnellboote* – fast boats (commonly referred to as E-Boats) – of 3.Schnellbootflottille. Flotilla commander, Kapitänleutnant Friedrich Kemnade, was tasked with establishing between 20 and 30 minefields off Grand Harbour. Operating out of Augusta, on the east coast of Sicily, Kemnade's force had to negotiate, at night, more than 100 miles (161km) to Malta, place mines at pre-determined locations and then withdraw, all without being detected. This involved stealth and excellent navigational skills, incorporating good use of charts and echo sounding equipment.

The first operation took place in mid-December 1941 and involved four boats (*S 33*, *S 35*, *S 61* and *S 31*) laden with different types of sea mines. Minefields (designated MT1A and MT1B) were to be placed north-east of Grand Harbour, with the nearest just 1,200 yards (1,100m) from the outer mole at the port entrance. The boats departed Augusta at 16:30hrs. Air cover was provided by two Italian fighters as far as Cape Passero, south-east Sicily.

As they neared Malta, the boats powered down to one engine, minimizing the sound of their approach (all boats were fitted with exhausts designed to reduce both noise and smoke emission). They proceeded in single line and at 22:10hrs stopped and waited for a diversionary air attack. This produced

German offshore minelaying operations, 1941–42

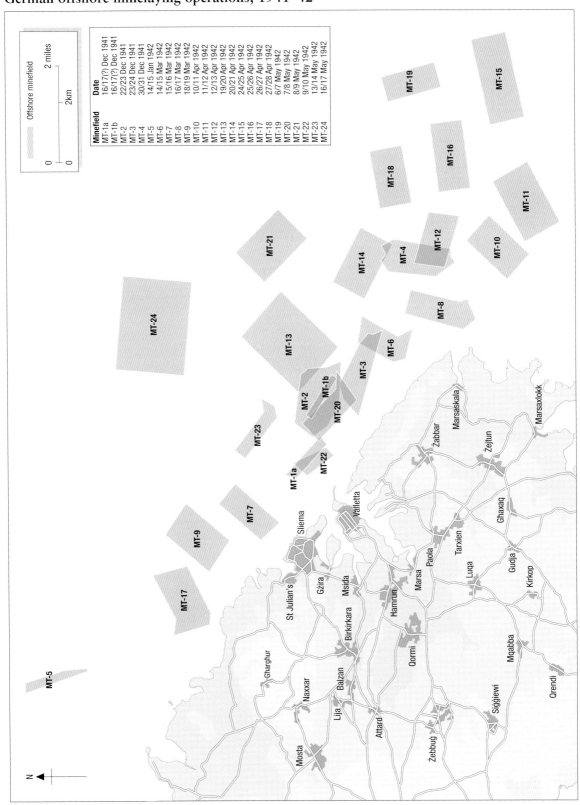

Minefield	Date
MT-1a	16/17(?) Dec 1941
MT-1b	16/17(?) Dec 1941
MT-2	22/23 Dec 1941
MT-3	23/24 Dec 1941
MT-4	30/31 Dec 1941
MT-5	14/15 Jan 1942
MT-6	14/15 Mar 1942
MT-7	15/16 Mar 1942
MT-8	16/17 Mar 1942
MT-9	18/19 Mar 1942
MT-10	10/11 Apr 1942
MT-11	11/12 Apr 1942
MT-12	12/13 Apr 1942
MT-13	19/20 Apr 1942
MT-14	20/21 Apr 1942
MT-15	24/25 Apr 1942
MT-16	25/26 Apr 1942
MT-17	26/27 Apr 1942
MT-18	27/28 Apr 1942
MT-19	6/7 May 1942
MT-20	7/8 May 1942
MT-21	8/9 May 1942
MT-22	9/10 May 1942
MT-23	13/14 May 1942
MT-24	16/17 May 1942

Offshore minefield

2 miles

2km

N

the desired effect, resulting in searchlights and coast watchers to turn their attention skyward, enabling the boats to approach unseen. At 23:00hrs the sound of aircraft was again heard. This time, a raider was illuminated by searchlights and targeted by AA guns. Kemnade's men seized the opportunity to place their mines, completing the job at 23:55hrs, just as the air raid ended. The boats withdrew to a point three nautical miles north of the harbour and there waited for opportunity targets and also to cover an Axis convoy en route via the Strait of Sicily to supply the Afrikakorps in North Africa. After an uneventful few hours, the boats returned to base, arriving after daybreak. Subsequent missions would follow a similar pattern, but not all would be as straightforward.

At the end of January 1942, 3.Schnellbootflottille was brought up to strength with the arrival from Wilhelmshaven of five more boats. Kemnade's activities continued, notwithstanding a persisting problem with self-detonating mines. It was surmised that the depth setting mechanism was faulty (another possibility is that mines had been sabotaged). Whatever the cause, by mid-April, the problem seems to have been rectified, allowing operations to proceed well into spring 1942.

SPITFIRES JOIN BATTLE

On Saturday morning, 7 March, four Beaufighter night fighters arrived on detachment from 89 Squadron in Egypt. These welcome additions would initially operate with 1435 Flight. At the same time, 700 miles (1,127km) to the west of Malta, another reinforcement operation was underway, as 15 Spitfire Mark VBs left the flight deck of the carrier *Eagle*. These, the first such fighters to see overseas service, had the speed and manoeuvrability to take on the latest Bf 109 F and the necessary firepower to destroy the Ju 88.

Pilots selected for Operation 'Spotter' were a cosmopolitan group hailing from Britain, Australia, New Zealand and Rhodesia. They – and their crated Spitfires – had departed England the previous month on board MV *Cape Hawke*. At Gibraltar, pilots and aircraft were transferred to the carrier HMS *Eagle*, following which, the Spitfires were assembled and made ready. The operation did not go quite as planned. After *Eagle* had departed Gibraltar and was en route eastward, a fault was discovered with the Spitfires' auxiliary 90-gallon fuel tanks. The carrier and escorting warships were compelled to return to Gibraltar. There was a delay of some days before the problem was rectified and the convoy again set sail. Guided by Blenheims from Gibraltar, all 15 Spitfires reached Malta safely, where they were allocated to 249 Squadron. Three days later, the new fighters were combat-ready.

In March 1942, Malta's Hurricanes were joined by the first Spitfire Vs, a machine that was more than capable of dealing with the Messerschmitt Bf 109 F in combat. These are Spitfires of 249 Squadron at Ta' Qali in mid-1942.

Tuesday, 10 March 1942: Shortly before 07:00hrs, the all clear announced the end of an all-night alert. An hour later, two enemy fighters approached, stopping short of crossing the coast. The next alarm was followed by an attack involving three Ju 88s. On both occasions no fighters were airborne and neither did AA open fire. At 10:12hrs, seven Spitfires were scrambled in response to an imminent attack, again by three Ju 88s escorted by Bf 109 fighters. Eight Hurricanes of 126 Squadron and four of 185 also took to the air. In the ensuing action, Flight Lieutenant Philip Heppell, flying a Spitfire, was credited with shooting down a Messerschmitt that crashed into the sea. AA was also credited with the destruction of a Bf 109, and several were claimed as probably destroyed or damaged. In the event, Feldwebel Heinz Rahlmeier of 8./Jagdgeschwader 53 was lost. Unteroffizier Hans Schade of the same unit was credited with the destruction of a Hurricane. The pilot, Australian Sergeant Jack Mayall of 126 Squadron was killed. Another Hurricane pilot escaped without injury after crash landing.

There would be 11 air raid warnings before midnight. The last daytime alert, which began in the late afternoon, continued for nearly two hours and involved an estimated 40 enemy aircraft. Four Spitfires intercepted, together with eight Hurricanes of 242 Squadron and three of 605. The *Kommandeur* of II./Jagdgeschwader 3, Hauptmann Karl-Heinz Krahl, succeeded in shooting down one Spitfire. Pilot Officer Ken Murray, another Australian, baled out but was severely injured. He died in hospital.

Numbers 242 and 605 squadrons ceased to exist on Malta from the 18th. The pilots were redistributed between the two Hurricane squadrons at Luqa (126) and Ħal Far (185). No. 249 Squadron with Spitfires remained at Ta' Qali. This had not gone unnoticed by the Luftwaffe. A new strategy was implemented with the initial aim of destroying RAF aircraft on the ground, beginning with Ta' Qali, before focusing on Luqa, Ħal Far and the seaplane base at Kalafrana and finally concentrating on targets in the area of Grand Harbour.

The new offensive began on Friday, 20 March. There were four daytime alerts, the first of which was the most destructive: a series of attacks continuing for five hours. About 20 Ju 88s arrived at intervals escorted by Bf 109 fighters. Bombs fell in the areas of Valletta, St Julian's Bay and Ħamrun. According to initial reports, six civilians and two soldiers were killed and about 50 more were injured, nearly all of them civilians.

Sixteen fighters were scrambled: four Spitfires providing top cover for 12 Hurricanes. AA guns also engaged. At least one Bf 109 was shot down and one Spitfire was lost. Neither pilot survived.

In the afternoon, Bf 109s accompanied a reconnaissance Ju 88 and three Bf 109s and a flying boat conducted a search, probably for the missing Bf 109 pilot. Soon after 18:15hrs, four Ju 88s escorted by nine fighters bombed Ta' Qali. AA fired, albeit without result. Ten minutes after the all clear, another heavy raid got underway,

Ground crew ('erks') responsible for Spitfire 'T' of 185 Squadron at Ħal Far in mid-1942.

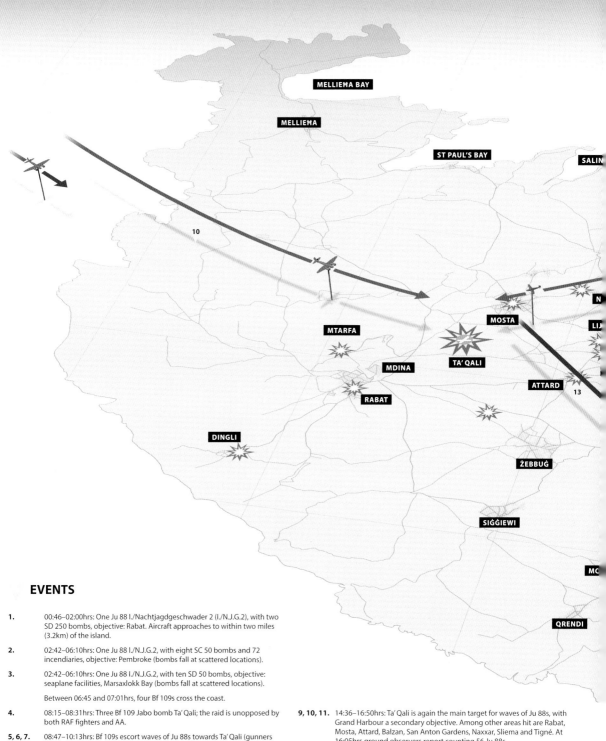

MELLIEĦA BAY

MELLIEĦA

ST PAUL'S BAY

SALIN

10

MTARFA

MOSTA

LIJ

N

TA' QALI

MDINA

ATTARD

13

RABAT

DINGLI

ŻEBBUĠ

SIĠĠIEWI

MO

QRENDI

EVENTS

1. 00:46–02:00hrs: One Ju 88 I./Nachtjagdgeschwader 2 (I./N.J.G.2), with two SD 250 bombs, objective: Rabat. Aircraft approaches to within two miles (3.2km) of the island.

2. 02:42–06:10hrs: One Ju 88 I./N.J.G.2, with eight SC 50 bombs and 72 incendiaries, objective: Pembroke (bombs fall at scattered locations).

3. 02:42–06:10hrs: One Ju 88 I./N.J.G.2, with ten SD 50 bombs, objective: seaplane facilities, Marsaxlokk Bay (bombs fall at scattered locations).

Between 06:45 and 07:01hrs, four Bf 109s cross the coast.

4. 08:15–08:31hrs: Three Bf 109 Jabo bomb Ta' Qali; the raid is unopposed by both RAF fighters and AA.

5, 6, 7. 08:47–10:13hrs: Bf 109s escort waves of Ju 88s towards Ta' Qali (gunners also report spotting nine Dorniers). Bombs also fall at Mtarfa military hospital, Rabat, Mosta, Lija, near Dingli, St Julian's, Manoel Island, Bighi and Corradino. No RAF fighters are scrambled; AA gunners claim one Ju 88 destroyed.

8. 11:07–14:32hrs: Continuation of bombing attacks on Ta' Qali. Eight Bf 110s, escorted by Bf 109s, raid the airfield and are met by five Hurricanes of 185 Squadron. At least one Bf 110 is shot down north of Malta.

9, 10, 11. 14:36–16:50hrs: Ta' Qali is again the main target for waves of Ju 88s, with Grand Harbour a secondary objective. Among other areas hit are Rabat, Mosta, Attard, Balzan, San Anton Gardens, Naxxar, Sliema and Tigné. At 16:05hrs ground observers report counting 56 Ju 88s.

12. 19:45–22:15hrs: At about 20:18hrs a single Ju 88 of I./N.J.G.2 approaches with eight SC 50 bombs and 72 incendiaries. Objective is apparently Safi strips. Instead, incendiaries fall in countryside near Benghisa and Attard.

13. 19:45–22:15hrs: One aircraft of I./N.J.G.2 crosses the coast, objective: Luqa. Bombs are instead dropped near Rabat and in the sea. Unopposed by fighters or AA.

LUFTWAFFE AIR OPERATIONS, 21 MARCH 1942

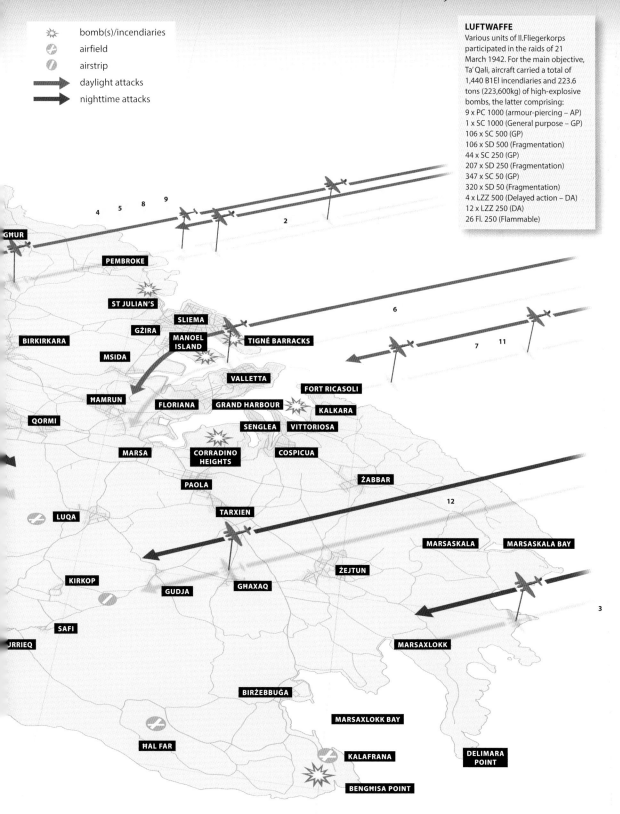

✳ bomb(s)/incendiaries
◉ airfield
◐ airstrip
➤ daylight attacks
➤ nighttime attacks

LUFTWAFFE
Various units of II.Fliegerkorps participated in the raids of 21 March 1942. For the main objective, Ta' Qali, aircraft carried a total of 1,440 B1El incendiaries and 223.6 tons (223,600kg) of high-explosive bombs, the latter comprising:
9 x PC 1000 (armour-piercing – AP)
1 x SC 1000 (General purpose – GP)
106 x SC 500 (GP)
106 x SD 500 (Fragmentation)
44 x SC 250 (GP)
207 x SD 250 (Fragmentation)
347 x SC 50 (GP)
320 x SD 50 (Fragmentation)
4 x LZZ 500 (Delayed action – DA)
12 x LZZ 250 (DA)
26 Fl. 250 (Flammable)

GĦUR
PEMBROKE
ST JULIAN'S
SLIEMA
GŻIRA
MANOEL ISLAND
TIGNÉ BARRACKS
BIRKIRKARA
MSIDA
VALLETTA
FORT RICASOLI
HAMRUN
FLORIANA
GRAND HARBOUR
KALKARA
QORMI
SENGLEA
VITTORIOSA
MARSA
CORRADINO HEIGHTS
COSPICUA
PAOLA
ŻABBAR
LUQA
TARXIEN
MARSASKALA
MARSASKALA BAY
KIRKOP
GĦAXAQ
ŻEJTUN
GUDJA
SAFI
JRRIEQ
MARSAXLOKK
BIRŻEBBUĠA
MARSAXLOKK BAY
ĦAL FAR
KALAFRANA
DELIMARA POINT
BENGĦISA POINT

4   5   8   9
2
6
7   11
12
3

German fighter pilots at their base in Sicily after a mission to Malta in late March 1942. The central figure is Major Herbert Kaminski, *Gruppenkommandeur* of I./Jagdgeschwader 53.

continuing until 23:35hrs. Ta' Qali was targeted by approximately 50 Ju 88s, which dropped incendiaries and high explosive bombs and machine-gunned the airfield and surrounding district. Naxxar, Mosta, Żebbuġ and Attard all suffered, with resultant civilian casualties.

Attacks continued in the form of nuisance raids throughout the night and on into the next day (21st). There was a brief alert at 06:45hrs, when four enemy fighters crossed the coast. Between 08:15 and 08:38hrs, three Bf 109s dropped bombs in the Ta' Qali area. Minutes later, the sirens sounded again, this time for an estimated 50 to 70 Ju 88s escorted by fighters. Ta' Qali airfield was the primary objective. AA was credited with shooting down one Ju 88 and damaging two more.

Emboldened, perhaps, by meeting with no aerial opposition, between 11:07 and 14:32hrs, Bf 109s patrolled over and around Malta while eight Bf 110s bombed Ta' Qali. On this occasion, however, Hurricanes of 185 Squadron were scrambled. Five Bf 110s were claimed as destroyed (including one by AA) and another as damaged.

At 14:36hrs, Ta' Qali was again targeted during a raid lasting more than two hours and involving 70 or more Ju 88s. This time, AA gunners, provided the sole defence, claimed three Ju 88s destroyed and three more damaged. Initial reports indicated that 135 civilians were killed, seriously injured, or buried under debris. At Gafa Street in Mosta, 24 people died and nearly twice as many were injured when the ceiling of a rock shelter collapsed. A Royal Australian Air Force officer, five RAF officers and a civilian also perished when a bomb landed next to the Point de Vue hotel at Rabat.

Notwithstanding RAF and AA claims, actual Luftwaffe casualties appear to have been comparatively light: A Bf 110 crashed into the sea north of Malta and a Ju 88 was lost in undisclosed circumstances. Both crews were posted missing. Three of the crew were taken prisoner when another Ju 88 was shot down near Ta' Qali.

The onslaught by II.Fliegerkorps on 20 and 21 March was such that Ta' Qali was rendered temporarily unserviceable. During this time, reinforcement flights continued. Nine Spitfires flew in from the carrier *Eagle* during Operation 'Picket I' on the 21st, followed by seven more ('Picket II') eight days later. On the 27th, Malta's fighter force was further strengthened, ten cannon-armed Hurricane IICs of 229 Squadron being detached from North Africa, with others following in April.

'M.W.10'

In the eastern Mediterranean, another convoy ('M.W.10') was underway. As a preliminary measure, the Fifth Destroyer Flotilla left Alexandria on Thursday morning, 19 March, to carry out anti-submarine sweeps as far as

Tobruk, before a rendezvous with the convoy at dawn on the 21st. During this phase, HMS *Heythrop* was torpedoed and sunk by *U.652*.

HMS *Breconshire* and the steamships *Clan Campbell*, *Pampas* and *Talabot* left Alexandria on 20 March, escorted by the cruiser *Carlisle* and six destroyers, the Fifteenth Cruiser Squadron and four destroyers following in the evening. By Sunday morning (22nd) all ships were in company, being joined two hours later by Force K from Malta (cruiser *Penelope* and destroyer *Legion*). Enemy air attacks commenced soon afterwards, continuing with increasing intensity throughout the day, with 124 sorties by bombers and reconnaissance machines and 12 by Italian torpedo-bombers.

In the early hours of the 22nd, the submarine *P 36* had reported the sailing of Italian warships from Taranto. These were sighted by *Euralyus* during the afternoon. Leaving a small force with the convoy, which now steered away, Rear Admiral Philip L. Vian, commanding Fifteenth Cruiser Squadron in *Cleopatra*, set in motion a pre-arranged plan. Cruisers and Fleet destroyers were detailed to concentrate on their leaders by divisions on a northerly course, before creating an easterly smoke screen. Gun action commenced just after 14:35hrs. Vian headed directly towards the enemy, at this stage comprising the heavy cruisers *Gorizia* and *Trento*, light cruiser *Giovanni delle Bande Nere* and four destroyers. The Fleet Commander, on board the battleship *Littorio*, was near to hand with several more destroyers. After a brisk action, he called for the Italian force to assemble around his flagship, thereby suspending the action.

With the immediate danger having been averted, the convoy continued on a westerly course. More than an hour passed before the next contact. Vian employed the same tactics as before, cruisers and destroyers steering easterly and westerly courses to lay smoke, while the convoy took evasive action by turning south. The ferocity of the ensuing engagement may be ascertained from the amount of ammunition expended, *Cleopatra* alone firing 1,000 rounds at low angle (ship to ship). The Italian fleet broke contact that evening. *Littorio* had been damaged and two destroyers failed to reach port: *Lanciere* and *Scirocco* foundering in rough seas and sinking with nearly all hands. HMS *Cleopatra* and three British destroyers had been damaged by shellfire, *Havock* and *Kingston* proceeding to Malta for repairs and *Lively* going to Tobruk.

By the 23rd, 'M.W.10' was within range of covering aircraft from Malta. *Talabot* and *Pampas* entered Grand Harbour that morning. *Breconshire*, with just eight miles (13km) to go, was bombed and immobilized and obliged to anchor off Żonqor Point (east Malta). The slowest ship, *Clan Campbell*, was still some 50 miles (80km) from harbour, escorted by the destroyer *Eridge*. Singled out by enemy aircraft later that morning, the merchantman was bombed and sunk. *Eridge* picked up 112 survivors. HMS *Legion*, ordered to join *Eridge*, was damaged

Included in spite of its poor quality is this rare photograph of the Norwegian steamer *Talabot* during a bombing attack at Grand Harbour in late-March 1942. (Norsk Maritimt Museum)

by a near miss, as was another destroyer, *Avon Vale* (the latter remaining out of commission for 14 weeks). *Breconshire* was eventually secured to a buoy in Marsaxlokk Bay after being towed there by HM Tug *Ancient*, but not before the destroyer *Southwold*, which had been assisting, hit a mine and was lost, together with five of her crew. 'M.W.10' had been a costly operation, but so far could still be considered a success. However, for as long as they were at Malta, the three supply vessels remained at risk from air attack. Unloading cargo should have been a priority, and yet there seems to have been no rush to complete the task.

Now, the Luftwaffe redirected its efforts. Within days, all three supply ships were written off: *Breconshire* overturned in Marsaxlokk Bay; *Pampas* settled at the stern on the harbour bottom; *Talabot* was set on fire and scuttled to prevent an explosion. She settled on an even keel, with her deck just above the waterline. Additional losses included the already-damaged submarine *P 39* and destroyer *Legion*.

Ultimately, 'MW10' only marginally improved the supply situation. Much of the precious fuel oil brought to Malta by *Breconshire* was pumped out, but only about 5,000 tons – a third of the cargo – could be saved from *Talabot* and *Pampas*. Malta's population was slowly starving and without a further resupply there was little possibility of the island holding out.

APRIL, 1942

Day and night raids were now a matter of routine. The number of daily alerts had lessened, but there was a noticeable increase in both the strength and weight of attacks. The main targets were the dockyard area and the airfields. More attention, too, was being paid to HAA gun positions.

Off Stromboli, on 1 April, *Urge* of the Tenth Submarine Flotilla torpedoed and sank the Italian cruiser *Giovanni delle Bande Nere* with the loss of half of the ship's company. The same day, at Malta, another British submarine, *Pandora*, had not yet finished unloading after a supply run when she was bombed and sunk at Hamilton Wharf; many of the crew went down with her. At nearby Lazzaretto, the submarine *P 36* was written off, fortunately without loss of life. A third submarine, *Unbeaten*, together with a number of vessels, including the minesweeper *Abingdon*, were damaged, and the minesweeping drifter *Sunset* was sunk.

Grand Harbour with the beached wreck of HMS *Gallant* (foreground) and scuttled *Talabot*.

On the 4th, the Greek submarine *Glaukos* was struck by three bombs and sank in Grand Harbour. The destroyer *Lance* was hit twice and *Penelope* was further damaged while in drydock. Next day, it was again the turn of Abingdon and the destroyer *Gallant* (under repair since January 1941); both were beached. In drydock, *Lance* received a direct hit, was blown off the chocks and left partially submerged. Other victims included the destroyer *Kingston* and oiler *Plumleaf* (already damaged on 26 March). HMS *Havock* had also suffered during air raids

Leichter Kreuzer „Penelope" im Dock von La Valletta. MALTA.

4.4.42.

M. 1: 1300

Zerstörungen durch Bombentreffer

Einschlag einer 1000 kg -Bombe

Grand Harbour and the Dockyard area were prime targets for Italian and German bombers. This Luftwaffe aerial photograph taken on 4 April 1942 shows the damaged cruiser HMS *Penelope* in drydock. So severely was this ship holed by bomb splinters during this time that she was nicknamed HMS 'Pepperpot'. Nevertheless, she was able to sail from Malta. Less than two years later she was torpedoed and lost with more than 400 of her crew.

while at Grand Harbour. She was repaired sufficiently to enable onward passage for further repairs at Gibraltar. Next day, while attempting to avoid an enemy submarine, the destroyer ran aground at Tunisia. The ship's company were taken prisoner.

On 7 April, 272 enemy aircraft carried out a series of attacks on the Grand Harbour area and all three airfields in what German records described as the 'heaviest attack so far'. Of a total of 400 tons of high-explosive bombs, 280 tons fell on Valletta; among buildings damaged or destroyed was the city's opulent Opera House. Malta's defence was wholly reliant, not for the first or last time, on the gunners of the Royal Artillery and Royal Malta Artillery.

Penelope sustained yet more damage the following day, but nonetheless was able to slip away, reaching Gibraltar before going on to America to complete repairs. Having been holed by innumerable splinters, she would forever be remembered by the nickname HMS 'Pepperpot'. On the 11th, *Kingston* was declared a total loss. At sea a few days later, HM Submarine *Upholder* disappeared during a patrol.

Malta's contribution to the war effort was formally recognized on 15 April with the award of the George Cross by King George VI. It was the only time such an honour had been bestowed on a community. The Axis high command, in the meantime, was well aware of the situation facing Britain's beleaguered Mediterranean outpost.

Like the British, the Germans also had access to top-secret signals emanating from enemy sources, including situation reports sent from the American military attaché in Cairo to his superiors in Washington. In order for Britain to gain American support, Colonel Bonner F. Fellers was kept up to date by the British with detailed information about the war in the desert and with regard to Malta. That

Kingsway (today, Republic Street), seen from Porta Reale, entrance to the city of Valletta. Centre-right are the bombed ruins of the Opera House.

XHB 8 (PP. 66–67)

XHB 8 was a heavy anti-aircraft gun position located at Il-Mara, Benghisa, on the coast just south-east of Ħal Far airfield. 'Benny', as it was commonly referred to by British gunners, comprised four static 3.7-inch guns. These were manned by personnel of 5th Battery, 4th HAA Regiment. This is No. 1 gun crew during an alert. Four men (1) prepare shells for a rapid reload. One man (2) prepares to fire, while another (3) sees to elevating and traversing the gun. Due to its location, XHB 8 was one of the most heavily bombed sites on Malta. In March 1943, Lance Bombardier Stan Fraser was transferred there from XHB 10 near Qrendi. He would write in his diary: 'There are more bomb craters within the boundary of this camp than any other on the island.'

Fellers was not exactly an Anglophile is evident from his reports, which often highlight the inadequacies and failures of British planning and strategy. Such information he dutifully despatched, using a code that had been compromised the year before before by Italian agents and shared with German intelligence. This security breach would not be identified until mid-1942. On 17 April, Fellers updated Washington – and unwittingly informed the Germans – about the situation on Malta, reporting that the island had already been abandoned as a base for surface vessels. Supplies would last for just seven weeks, he revealed.

Malta was at last afforded a respite in mid-April, when stormy conditions impeded Axis air operations for three days. Operation 'Calendar' followed, when, on 20 April, the American carrier *Wasp* ferried to a launch point west of Malta Spitfires of 601 (County of London) and 603 (City of Edinburgh) squadrons. An otherwise successful operation was marred by the death of one of the ship's servicing party, who was struck by a spinning propeller and killed, and of the loss of one aircraft, whose American pilot diverted to Algeria. The remaining 46 Spitfires arrived safely.

The Luftwaffe subjected Malta to a bombing campaign of varying intensity. This low-flying Ju 88 is shown over Għadira, probably on 25 April 1942.

The Luftwaffe responded with heavy attacks on the airfields, rendering Ta' Qali temporarily unserviceable, destroying a Hurricane, two Spitfires and a Blenheim and damaging a good number of aircraft. In the air, losses amounted to three Spitfires, at least one Bf 109 and two MC.202s. Two Spitfire pilots and one Macchi pilot were killed.

The next day, Malta's striking forces were reinforced by six Wellingtons of 148 Squadron from Egypt, two more aircraft following in due course. At the same time, it was decided that Malta could no longer be considered a secure haven for the Tenth Submarine Flotilla and before the end of the month the five surviving U-class boats were ordered to Alexandria. HM Submarine *Urge* never arrived – lost with all hands in Kemnade's minefields north of Grand Harbour.

In April, operational losses accounted for at least eight Hurricanes and 13 Spitfires and another Hurricane crashed while on an air test; some 74 aircraft, including 42 fighters and 22 Wellingtons, were destroyed on the ground. The Luftwaffe lost some 17 Bf 109s, eight Ju 87s, 11 Ju 88s, a Bf 110 and a Do. 24; the Italians at least three MC.202s and a BR.20M. In addition, many more Axis machines were damaged, some crashing on returning to base. Luftwaffe operations against Malta between 20 March and 28 April 1942 are stated to have totalled 11,819 sorties: 5,807 by bombers, 5,667 by fighters and 345 by reconnaissance aircraft. In this five-and-a-half-week period, the weight of bombs dropped is reported to have exceeded 6,557 tonnes.

Resupply operations by Axis sea transports were proceeding relatively unimpeded. In April the War Diary of the German Naval Staff, Operations Division (*Kriegstagebuch der Seekriegsleitung*) regularly noted that convoys to North Africa were proceeding according to plan and largely without incident. At the main Libyan ports of Tripoli and Benghazi, over 100,000 tons of cargo were unloaded – more than double that in March – another 2,386 tons were unloaded at Derna, this in addition to deliveries by tankers and colliers.

'C3'/'HERKULES'

Towards the end of April, the Luftwaffe in Sicily prepared to redeploy aircraft north for the spring offensive in Russia, and south to support Rommel in Libya. Attacks on Malta would continue with Italian aircraft and a reduced German force. These developments occurred just as Allied aerial reconnaissance photographs revealed what appeared to be satellite airfields under construction in Sicily. It was assumed that they were to accommodate gliders for the anticipated Axis invasion of Malta. The Italians had long been in favour of such an undertaking; the Germans less so. But by February 1942, Kesselring was in agreement with Italian senior officers that Malta was key to success in North Africa, an idea propounded by Grossadmiral Erich Raeder and supported by Rommel. Codenamed 'C3' by the Italians and '*Herkules*' by the Germans, the operation was scheduled to take place in the summer.

'*C3*' was to have been an ambitious undertaking, involving nearly 100,000 men to be landed by air and sea. Generale Ugo Cavallero, Chief of Italy's *Comando Supremo*, would oversee the operation, with participating forces deploying under their respective commanders. Italian land forces included one parachute, one air-landing and five infantry divisions, a regiment of marines, four 'black shirt' militia battalions and a tank group. The German contribution to the ground offensive consisted of airborne units of 7.Flieger-Division. Transport and air support were a joint Italo-German responsibility. Italian warships would be available to escort landing craft and to provide supporting fire.

The initial phase of this most complex operation was designed primarily to neutralise Malta's defences with ongoing air attacks. This was expected to continue for nearly three weeks prior to the landings. Malta's southern region was then to be secured by airborne troops, preparatory to an assault on all three airfields so as to facilitate the arrival by air of additional forces and supplies. Amphibious landings would take place in the area of Marsaxlokk Bay, including a secondary assault with Forts Benghisa and Delimara as the main objectives, thus diverting defending forces from the main landing, and also to support troops in securing Marsaxlokk. In addition, there would be feints and demonstration attacks, together with airdrops of dummy parachutists in the north, concurrent with the arrival of paratroopers further south. At the same time, the lightly defended island of Gozo was to be secured for use as a logistics base.

Events faltered at the final planning and preparation stages. By June, when Rommel was making good progress in Libya, Hitler had lost what little enthusiasm he might have had. At the end of July, 'C3' was postponed indefinitely.

MAY, 1942

On 7 May, General Gort replaced Sir William Dobbie as the new Governor. Viscount Gort arrived at a critical period. Two days later, some 650 miles (1,046km) further west, HMS *Eagle* and USS *Wasp* prepared to fly off 64 Spitfires. One returned to

Probably apocryphal, but indicative of the seriousness of Malta's situation in mid-1942.

EXTRACT :- D.R.O's DATED 14.5.42
R.A.F. STATION, TA-KALI, MALTA

A GIBBET HAS BEEN ERECTED ON THE CORNER OF THE ROAD LEADING TO THE CAVES. ANY MAN, WOMAN OR CHILD, CIVILIAN OR SERVICE PERSONNEL, FOUND GUILTY OF SABOTAGE, THEFT, OR IN ANY OTHER WAY IMPEDING THE WAR EFFORT AND SUBSEQUENTLY SHOT, WILL BE HUNG FROM THIS GIBBET AS A WARNING TO ALL OTHERS.

10 May 1942: unloading supplies delivered by HMS *Welshman*

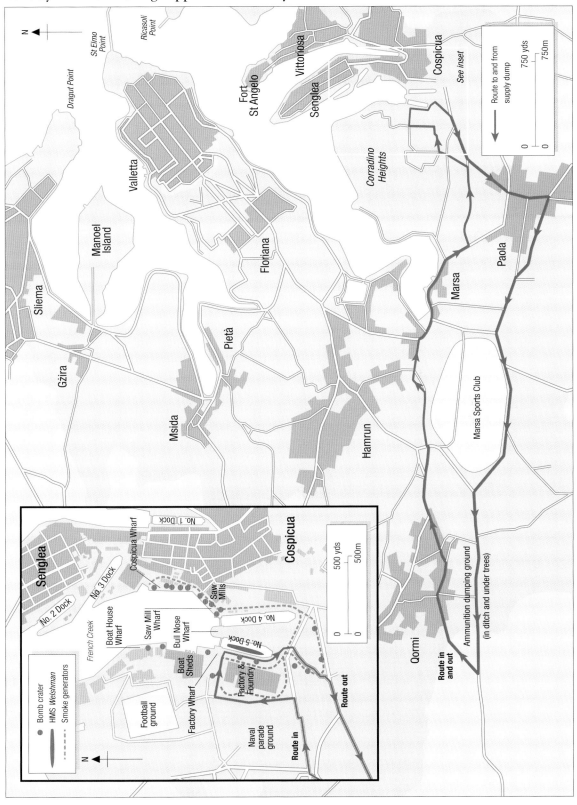

alight on *Wasp* with a faulty fuel system and of the remainder, 60 reached Malta. As the reinforcements neared their destination, available fighters were airborne to deter prowling Bf 109s. Some Spitfires were attacked as they came in to land, one pilot being fatally injured as a result.

Once safely on the ground, each Spitfire was met by a runner and directed to a dispersal pen where armourers, fitters, electricians and two assisting soldiers stood by with a prepared supply of tinned fuel, oil, glycol and ammunition. An experienced Malta pilot immediately took over the aircraft, ready to scramble.

AA ammunition restrictions (introduced as a result of shortages) had been lifted in anticipation of the expected enemy onslaught. Before restrictions were re-imposed on the 11th, the number of rounds expended would amount to 492 x 4.5-inch HE, 5,716 x 3.7-inch HE, 1,010 x 3-inch HE, 115 x 3.7-inch shrapnel, 57 x 3-inch shrapnel and 6,036 x 40mm.

Air attacks continued the following day (10th), by which time, however, Axis bombers had another target. The fast minelayer-cruiser HMS *Welshman*, disguised as a French destroyer so as to mislead enemy forces (a ruse employed previously with her sister ship *Manxman*), reached Grand Harbour that morning to disembark 117 mainly RAF personnel. She also brought supplies, including nearly 82,000 Bofors rounds and 1,268 smoke-producing generators.

In Malta, there were already seven tons of smoke contained in 92 generators. These were positioned around *Welshman* at distances of between 100 and 200 yards (91.5 to 183m) in time for the first daylight bombing raid. On a signal from Fighter Control, half were ignited, providing a screen that effectively shielded the vessel from the air for 12 minutes, whereupon the other half were ignited. Unloading of *Welshman* was completed by 13:00hrs. The used generators were replaced in time for the next assault, which came about an hour later. Grand Harbour was targeted one more time that day. *Welshman*, although damaged by near misses, was able to depart Malta that night. Smoke was used for the first time on 10 May and, in conjunction with an effective AA barrage and interception of enemy aircraft by RAF fighters, was a proven success.

In two days, six civilians and 20 military personnel, including five fighter pilots, had lost their lives. Seven Spitfires had been shot down and one unserviceable Wellington had been destroyed. Axis losses included two Italian and 12 German machines; 27 Axis aircrew were dead and two were prisoners of war. The next day's *Times of Malta* headlines said it all: 'Battle of Malta: Axis Heavy Losses', with sub-headings praising the efforts of the RAF and AA. Exultant commanders added to the mood with their own congratulatory messages. There was to be much hard fighting before the end of the siege, but 10 May 1942 is considered as a turning point in a battle that had already lasted nearly two years.

Spitfires still awaiting delivery at Gibraltar were ferried by HMS *Eagle* to within flying range of Malta on the 18th. A few days later, Wellington bombers and torpedo-carriers began to arrive on detachment from Egypt. With sufficient Spitfires to hand, surviving fighter pilots of 229 Squadron departed with their Hurricanes. (Three failed to arrive; two pilots became prisoners of war, the other evaded capture.)

Meanwhile, German aircraft continued to be redeployed from Sicily. By the last week in May, the only Bf 109 units remaining were the Stab and II.Gruppe of Jagdgeschwader 53. Some bombers and other aircraft types also remained. Italian machines transferred from the mainland helped make up for the deficit. An increasing number of missions were flown by Italians, but, typically, these lacked the tenacity of those carried out by German aircrew.

In May, Axis ships reaching North African ports from Italy transported more 2,262 vehicles (including tanks) and nearly 1,000 men. In all, up to 61,610 tons of freight were unloaded at Benghazi, 83,110 tons at Tripoli, and a further 7,474 tons of German army materiel at Derna. Axis convoys began to suffer towards the end of the month, however, with the sinking of at least four steamers and an Italian destroyer.

The Royal Navy had also fared badly in May, losing HM Ships *Lively*, *Kipling* and *Jackal* within two days. More than 600 survivors were rescued by *Jervis*, the only destroyer to return to Alexandria.

3.SCHNELLBOOTFLOTTILLE

On 3 May, Kapitänleutnant Friedrich Kemnade of 3.Schnellbootflottille had attended a meeting in Rome to discuss a deployment to the eastern Mediterranean towards the end of the month in support of a German offensive in Libya. In the meantime, mining operations off Malta continued. Minefield MT19 was put in place during the night of 6/7 May. On completion of the task, all three boats (*S 31*, *S 34* and *S 61*) withdrew and then waited for opportunity targets. Soon, a vessel came into view. HM Motor Launch *130*, on a routine patrol, stood little chance. Approaching from behind, Kemnade's boats closed to about 330 yards (300m) before opening fire with 20mm cannons and machine guns. According to Kemnade, the British were taken completely by surprise, and it was several minutes before they returned fire.

According to the Royal Navy, the first fusillade set the ML on fire and both engines were stopped. The commanding officer, Lieutenant David R. H. Jolly, and First Lieutenant Frederick Price-Fox were wounded. They, together with two wounded ratings, manned the boat's aft Oerlikon and forward 3-pdr. Only when the ML was ablaze from stem to stern, did Jolly give the order to abandon ship. Eleven of the crew were transferred to *S 31*. Three ratings had lost their lives and a fourth died later in hospital. One German seaman had received a minor head wound. After a hurried search of the vessel, explosive charges were placed and just after 03:00hrs, detonated.

Photo-montage of *Schnellboot S 31* sunk off Grand Harbour in May 1942. (underwatermalta.org)

Malta Infantry Brigade areas and main military establishments in May 1942

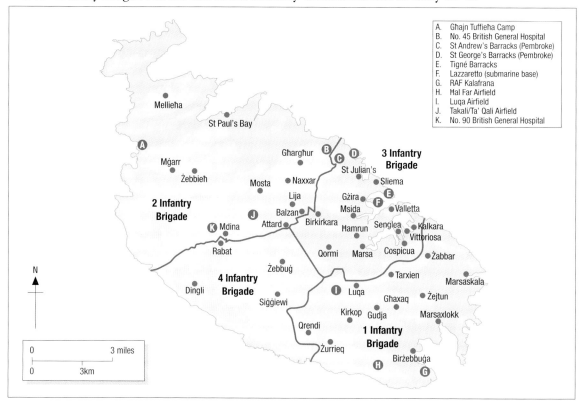

A. Ghajn Tuffieha Camp
B. No. 45 British General Hospital
C. St Andrew's Barracks (Pembroke)
D. St George's Barracks (Pembroke)
E. Tigné Barracks
F. Lazzaretto (submarine base)
G. RAF Kalafrana
H. Hal Far Airfield
I. Luqa Airfield
J. Takali/Ta' Qali Airfield
K. No. 90 British General Hospital

To the amazement of Kemnade, Malta's defences did not react then, or as his force withdrew. In fact, Malta's coast defences had been put on alert two minutes after the first bout of firing. For whatever reason, no further action was taken.

May 1942 was to be especially eventful for 3.Schnellbootflottille. During the night of the 9th, seven boats proceeded to a point off Grand Harbour. One group was to intercept HMS *Welshman*, known to be en route from Gibraltar. Another group was to lay mines; in the event *S 31* struck a mine placed previously and was blown up. *S 61* took on board survivors before the two remaining boats withdrew. E-Boats of the other group went on to engage what were described as a fishing steamer and escorting patrol vessel north of Marsaskala, reporting that the former had been sunk and the latter set on fire – these were, in fact, the trawler *Beryl* and drifter *Trusty Star*, both of which returned safely to port. *Welshman* was not attacked and after cutting two mines had entered Grand Harbour at 05:25hrs.

3.Schnellbootflottille carried out its 24th mining operation in the early hours of 16/17 May. Searchlights illuminated all four boats when they were still several miles offshore. Coastal batteries engaged, immediately immobilising *S 34*. Other boats attempted to lay a smoke screen, while the crew were rescued and an unsuccessful attempt made to blow up the severely damaged vessel. Three men had died and several were wounded, one of them seriously. *S 34* was later sunk by a pair of Bf 109s, one of which was shot down, resulting in the death of the pilot. 3.Schnellbootflottille had been well

Heavy anti-aircraft gun positions in May 1942

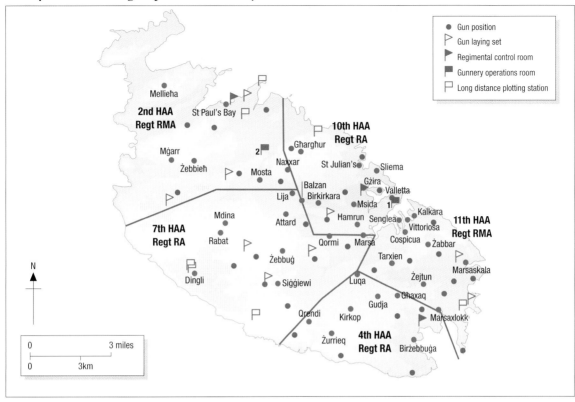

and truly compromised and would not operate off Malta again, but for a brief period in November 1942.

German minefields would continue to take toll of Allied vessels. The submarine *Olympus* was lost on 8 May shortly after leaving Grand Harbour following a delivery run from Gibraltar. Of the 98 on board, among them personnel of submarines sunk at Malta, just nine survived. Minesweeping was especially hazardous. While returning from such an operation in the early hours of 11 May, the tug *C 308* detonated a mine, resulting in the deaths of nine of her crew. On the 26th, eight were reported missing when the drifter *Eddy* hit a mine while en route to port (one of two who were injured died in hospital); four days later, another tug, *St Angelo*, was blown up with the loss of four hands while sweeping off Grand Harbour.

AXIS CLANDESTINE OPERATIONS

Both sides were involved in clandestine operations, the scope and scale of which are still undisclosed. Certainly, British submarines from Malta were involved as early as February 1941, going on to land and pick up agents and commandos.

Tasks carried out by Axis seaborne units included close reconnaissance of Malta's shore defences. On Monday morning, 18 May 1942, an operation took place involving the Italian *MAS Abba* and a detachment of smaller vessels in support of *MTSM 218* (*motoscafo da turismo silurante*

On 8 May 1942, Unteroffizier Heinrich Becker of 8./Jagdgeschwader 53 was shot down for the second time in less than a fortnight. Previously he had been rescued after baling out and landing in the sea. This time Becker was taken prisoner. His Bf 109 crashed at Marsa Sports Club.

modificato – a two-man torpedo assault craft) crewed by tenente Giuseppe Cosulich and sottocapo Aldo Pia, and *MTSM 214* with sottotenente Ongarillo Ungarelli and sottocapo Arnaldo de Angeli.

Palombaro (Diver) Giuseppe Guglielmo of Xª Flottiglia MAS was taken on *MTSM 218* to Marsaskala Bay. There, he entered the water and, with the aid of a flotation device, paddled inshore, making a mental note of anything of importance. He then decided to have a closer look and clambered ashore. Unfortunately for Guglielmo, when the time came to exfiltrate, he was unable to relocate the *MTSM*. Cosulich waited for him until dawn, before withdrawing. Guglielmo, still in his diving suit, eventually surrendered to a Maltese fisherman.

As these events were being played out, on the south coast, *MTSM 214* disembarked a Maltese Fascist turned spy, sottotenente Carmelo Borg Pisani. The spot chosen could not have been worse. Borg Pisani was quite unable to scale the sheer cliff below which he had been put ashore. He was discovered on 20 May, went on to face trial and was hanged. He was posthumously awarded the *medaglia d'oro al valor militare*, Italy's highest award for bravery.

OPERATION 'JULIUS'

The first and only time that a Spitfire delivery flight was successfully intercepted by enemy fighters was on 3 June. Of 31 fighters that took off from HMS *Eagle*, four failed to arrive. Another crashed on landing. Just six days later, the same carrier delivered 32 more Spitfires. Among the arrivals was Canadian, Sergeant George 'Screwball' Beurling. Assigned to 249 Squadron, Beurling would run up a string of victories, being credited with 26 aircraft destroyed (in addition to two Focke-Wolfe Fw 190s claimed over Europe). By the time he was shot down and wounded in October 1942 he had become his country's – and Malta's – leading fighter ace.

In June, there were two simultaneous attempts to supply Malta. Operation 'Julius' comprised convoys 'M.W.11' ('Vigorous') and 'G.M.4' ('Harpoon'), the former west-bound with 11 cargo ships and the latter east-bound with HMS *Welshman* (carrying supplies), five merchantmen and a tanker. Patrolling submarines and aircraft from Malta and North Africa were to support the undertaking.

Following the latest Spitfire delivery, Wellingtons of 104 Squadron departed to make way for supporting units for 'Julius'. The first of 15 Beauforts of 217 Squadron and 14 Beaufighters of 235 Squadron flew in from Gibraltar (one Beaufighter failed to arrive). The state of these aircraft and/or armaments was such that much maintenance had to be carried out before they could be put into service.

Meanwhile, from the Middle East came six Baltimores and six torpedo-carrying Wellingtons of 38 Squadron. By mid-June, serviceable aircraft stood at ten Wellingtons, 19 Beaufighters (including five night-fighters), 12 Beauforts, six Baltimores, 95 Spitfire fighters and three PRU machines and seven FAA aircraft (including ASV Swordfish and torpedo-bombers).

By May 1942, 236 aircraft pens had been constructed at airfields, together with 27 miles (43.5km) of dispersal track. This mammoth task had been achieved by all three branches of the armed forces, sometimes joined by Malta Police detachments and civilian labour, who were required to toil under the most oppressive weather conditions, while in constant danger of air attacks. To accommodate the additional aircraft, within days, a further 21 pens were erected at Luqa, with as many as 2,800 men working at any one time.

XHB 10 HAA gun position near Qrendi, during evening stand-to in June 1942.

In an attempt to lessen the risk posed to 'Vigorous', Luftwaffe airfields in Crete and Cyrenaica were targeted by the Special Air Service during the night of 13/14 June. In the area of Heraklion, 16 aircraft were destroyed. (The next day, 50 Cretans were shot in reprisal. A good number of the saboteurs were either killed or captured.)

'Vigorous', while under the command of Rear Admiral Vian, was to be directed jointly by Vice Admiral Sir Henry Harwood, C-in-C Mediterranean Fleet, and Air Marshal Sir Arthur W. Tedder, AOC-in-C RAF Middle East Command, from the headquarters of No. 201 (Naval Co-operation) Group. The operation seemed doomed from the very beginning. A diversionary task intended to lure the Regia Marina from its Italian bases, thus expending fuel on a wasted effort, failed when the Italians did not take the bait. When the Allied vessels, which included four of the 11 merchantmen, then attempted to rendezvous with the main convoy, they were attacked by German dive-bombers. *City of Calcutta* was damaged and detached to Tobruk. The remaining cargo ships joined the main convoy, which was further depleted when *Elizabeth Bakke* failed to keep up and had to withdraw. During the night of 13/14 June, rough seas necessitated the return to port of accompanying motor torpedo boats. *MTB 259* foundered and was lost. Another slow merchantman, *Aagtekirk*, was escorted to Tobruk, only to be attacked and sunk by enemy aircraft. During air attacks on Sunday, the 14th, *Bhutan* was lost and the corvette *Primula* damaged. In the meantime, a powerful Italian naval force was steaming southward to meet the convoy. In the early hours of the 15th, Vian received an order to abort and return to Alexandria. Meanwhile, German E-Boats of 3.Schnellbootflottille struck, torpedoing and damaging the cruiser *Newcastle* and the destroyer *Hasty*. *Hasty* could not be saved and was finished off by HMS *Hotspur*.

After an ineffectual night strike by Malta-based Wellingtons, Beaufort torpedo-bombers followed up with a dawn attack on the Italian Fleet, now some 200 miles (322km) north of the convoy. The cruiser *Trento* was severely damaged and subsequently torpedoed by the British submarine *Umbra* (*P 35*), sinking with the loss of nearly half of the ship's company. Not long afterwards, American B-24 Liberator bombers from Egypt struck, achieving one hit on the battleship *Littorio* (that night she was further damaged in a torpedo attack by Malta-based Wellingtons).

Believing that the threat from Italian naval forces had been averted, Harwood instructed Vian to again set course for Malta. When it was

Light anti-aircraft gun positions in June 1942

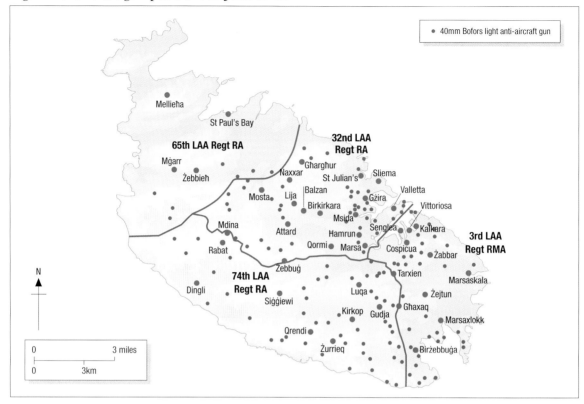

discovered that the Italian Fleet was, in fact, still en route, Vian was once more ordered to turn about. That afternoon, yet another command was received, again requiring the convoy to resume a heading for Malta. This, Vian wisely chose to ignore. Another signal effectively assigned further decision making to Vian, who continued eastward, overruling a final request to alter course that evening. With ammunition and fuel reserves dangerously low, there could be no other option.

Centurion (a decommissioned battleship employed as a decoy – and identified as such by the Germans), the British cruisers *Birmingham* and *Arethusa* and destroyers *Airedale* and *Nestor* had all been damaged during air attacks; both destroyers having to be sunk by friendly forces. While withdrawing eastward, the cruiser *Hermione* was torpedoed and sunk by *U.205*.

Vice Admiral Alban T. B. Curteis was responsible for 'Harpoon'. His covering force included two carriers, *Eagle* and *Argus*, with on-board Sea Hurricanes, Fulmars and Swordfish. The enemy was aware of 'Harpoon' soon after the ships had entered the Mediterranean on 12 June. Italian aircraft from Sardinia struck in the morning of the 14th. The cruiser HMS *Liverpool* and the Dutch cargo ship *Tanimbar* were hit by aerial torpedoes; the former withdrew and the latter was set on fire and lost. Air attacks resumed in the early evening, this time by Italian and German units from Sicily.

At about 20:00hrs, *Welshman* was detached to proceed to Malta. At 21:15hrs, the convoy separated, Force W, which included both carriers, returning to Gibraltar with Vice Admiral Curteis, while Force X under Captain Cecil C. Hardy, continued with the merchant ships towards Malta.

Searchlight positions in June 1942

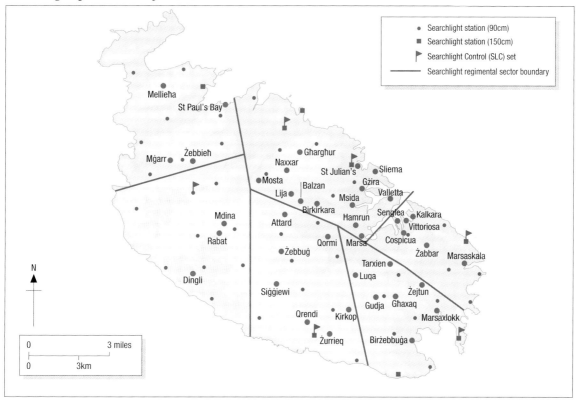

On Monday morning (15th), two Italian cruisers accompanied by destroyers were detected 15 miles (24km) to northward. Battle was joined at 06:40hrs. *Bedouin* and *Partridge* were both hit, the former being seriously damaged and having to be taken in tow by *Partridge*. *Cairo* was struck by shellfire, sustaining minor damage, before being hit by a dud, which resulted in the engine room becoming partially flooded. During an air attack, *Kentucky* was disabled and taken in tow by *Hebe*. *Chant* was bombed and sunk. But the Royal Navy did succeed in damaging the cruiser *Raimondo Montecuccoli* and a destroyer, *Ugolino Vivaldi*. From mid-morning, Malta-based fighters provided almost continuous air cover, but during a brief period when one group of Spitfires was in the process of being relieved, Ju 88s struck. *Burdwan* was near-missed and left disabled. Attempts to scuttle *Burdwan* and *Kentucky* were unsuccessful and both ships were eventually sunk by enemy forces. At 13:15hrs, there was another dive-bombing attack by Italian Ju 87s, once more occurring before relieving Spitfires had arrived. The Italian cruisers, in the meantime, had turned their attention to *Partridge* and the crippled *Bedouin*. At about 14:30hrs, S.79s arrived overhead and *Bedouin* was finally sunk by aerial torpedo.

During the day, it was the turn of the Italian warships to come under air attack, Malta-based aircraft harassing the force as it retired northward. Enemy air attacks also continued until, that night, *Troilus* at last reached Grand Harbour.

The last of victim of Kemnade's minefields had been *Trusty Star* on 10 June. Now, *Orari*, following close behind *Troilus*, detonated a mine, although she was able to continue. Two destroyers, *Matchless* and *Badsworth*,

Troops help with unloading cargo from a lighter following the arrival of *Orari* and *Troilus* in June 1942. Included are cartons of cooked sliced bacon, sacks of sugar, soap and RASC stores.

were also damaged; they would remain out of commission for 19 weeks and five months respectively. A minesweeper, *Hebe*, already damaged on the 15th, was also rendered ineffective. The Polish destroyer *Kujawiak* and Malta-based drifter *Justified* were sunk. The former went down with a number of her crew just east of Malta and there were three fatalities on the latter.

Many had paid with their lives for the delivery of two shiploads of supplies. Six Allied warships, one MTB and five merchantmen had been sunk and at least 12 warships were damaged. Including shipboard losses, but discounting those destroyed on the ground, more than 50 Axis and at least 37 Allied machines were written off.

Lessons had been learned from the failures of 'M.W.10' and unloading and dispersing the ships' cargo was now a priority. All fighters and an arrangement of AA barrages were made ready. Unloading was to be undertaken by naval and army personnel and Maltese stevedores, the infantry allocating about 2,300 men for working parties. In addition to unloading ships and transferring cargo from lighters to shore, infantry also provided firefighting crews and dockside labour, tally clerks, messengers and telephonists, manned first aid posts and a Docks Directorate (central headquarters). Smoke cover, the responsibility of the Royal Artillery, would help conceal operations from aerial view. Another 1,700 troops were stationed at airfields for servicing and refuelling aircraft, to assist armourers, fill bomb craters and for control and other duties. Fourteen Bren Carriers and two tanks were employed as tow vehicles. After a rehearsal on Saturday, 13 June, events got underway at 07:00hrs on Tuesday before concluding on Saturday evening, by which time 15,000 tons had been unloaded. During this period, neither the Italians nor Germans bombed the port area.

For the remainder of June, Malta-based aircraft continued with anti-shipping operations. On the 21st, Beauforts and escorting Beaufighters targeted a convoy near the Kerkennah Islands. At least two Beauforts failed to return, but the 7,744-ton *Reichenfels*, the last German steamer equipped with heavy derricks, was sunk, the War Diary of the German Naval Staff noting: 'It is proof of the danger to transports to North Africa as long as Malta has not been eliminated completely as an enemy base.' By the end of the month, smaller Italian steamers from Brindisi and Taranto were already taking a circuitous route to avoid Malta, entering the Aegean through the Corinth Canal, transhipping at Suda, if necessary, and then continuing to Libya.

On 21 June, Tobruk changed hands, falling to the Deutsches Afrikakorps (it would not be retaken until November). Number 601 Squadron was sent from Malta to join the hard-pressed RAF in North Africa. Towards the end of the month, bombers of Stab, II. and III./Kampfgeschwader 77 also began to redeploy to Sicily from the Eastern Front, soon to be followed by Bf 109s of I./Jagdgeschwader 77. The Axis situation was further improved, not least with the arrival on Sicily of three *squadriglie* of 20° Gruppo, 51° Stormo C.T. with new MC. 202s.

OPERATION 'PEDESTAL'

July began with a renewed Axis air offensive, which lessened in intensity, as events at the El Alamein front necessitated the temporary transfer of some Luftwaffe units. Bombing raids fell by 50 per cent in the second half of the month.

Air Vice-Marshal Keith Park arrived at this opportune time to take over as AOC from Air Vice-Marshal Lloyd. Park was dismayed to learn that during the first half of July, just 8 per cent of bombing raids on the airfields had been intercepted before the bombers reached their target. He promptly revised fighter defence procedure, implementing a forward interception plan, whereby raiders would be met before they reached Malta. The tactic duly became standard procedure, at times resulting in bombers jettisoning their load prematurely, and missions being aborted.

In the first two weeks of July, some 25 Spitfires and 19 pilots had been lost. Fourteen Spitfires were damaged. Losses were alleviated when HMS *Eagle* delivered 31 Spitfires on the 15th followed, less than a week later, by 28 more (one Spitfire crashed on take-off, resulting in the death of the pilot). These latest reinforcements enabled 1435 Flight, previously rendered ineffective as a Hurricane unit, to be reconstituted and equipped with Spitfires, being retitled 1435 Squadron soon afterwards.

During the month, neither side in the Mediterranean incurred heavy naval losses. Even so, the effect on Axis coastal shipping was particularly felt after three steamers were put out of commission. The German *Savona* had to be written off after running aground at the end of June, and in July Allied forces accounted for the German *Brook* and Italian *Sturla*. By the 18th, following the destruction by Allied aircraft of a fuel dump at Tobruk, the Axis supply situation was deemed critical.

It was no less dire for those on Malta. All now depended on the success or failure of the next convoy. At Scapa, Scotland, naval units had assembled, preparatory to the start of Operation 'Pedestal'. The convoy (designation 'W.S.21S') sailed from the Clyde during the night of 2/3 August, to rendezvous further south with other units. These would enter the Mediterranean, having been organized into forces under an all-encompassing Force F, commanded by Acting Vice Admiral Edward N. Syfret. Near the Skerki Channel, units would separate, one component continuing towards Malta as Force X, while the remainder of Force F, now operating as Force Z, returned to Gibraltar.

There were five aircraft carriers: *Furious* (with Spitfires destined for Malta: codename 'Bellows'), *Victorious*, *Argus*, *Eagle* and *Indomitable*, together with the battleships *Nelson* and *Rodney* and cruisers *Cairo*, *Nigeria*, *Kenya*, *Manchester*, *Phoebe*, *Sirius* and *Charybdis* and 30 destroyers. Two more destroyers were to escort from Malta the empty cargo ships *Troilus* and *Orari* (as Force Y). The 13 transports were *Empire Hope, Dorset, Wairangi, Rochester Castle, Waimarama, Brisbane Star, Port Chalmers, Almeria Lykes, Santa Elisa, Clan*

Detail from a Luftwaffe aerial photograph taken on 12 August during an attack that left the carrier *Indomitable* (1) severely damaged. Forty-eight were killed or died of their injuries; four pilots were lost and more than fifty all ranks were wounded. Cruiser (2) at centre is probably HMS *Charybdis*.

MACCHI C.202 SHOT DOWN AT GOZO (PP. 82–83)

Ta' Qali was bombed and rendered temporarily unserviceable during a raid on Monday morning, 27 July 1942. Nine Ju 88s were escorted towards Malta by German and Italian fighters. Eight Spitfires were already airborne from a previous alert. Additional Spitfires were scrambled as the raid approached. At least two Macchi C.202s were shot down, both by Canadian Sergeant George 'Screwball' Beurling of 249 Squadron. Capitano Furio Niclot Doglio, commander of 151ª Squadriglia C.T., was killed. Sergente Maggiore Faliero Gelli of 378ª Squadriglia C.T. crash-landed in a tiny field at Ta' Kuljat, Gozo. The injured pilot (1) was taken prisoner. The 'Cat and Mice' emblem of 51º Stormo C.T. (2) was later cut from the starboard side of the Macchi fuselage and the rudder (3) dismantled. Beurling would pose with these trophies for what would become the best-known photograph of Malta's top-scoring fighter ace (see page 93).

Ferguson, *Glenorchy*, *Melbourne Star* and *Deucalion* accompanied by the oil tanker *Ohio*.

The Axis command, realizing that an important convoy would soon be on its way eastward, hurriedly reinforced Italian and German air force units. The RAF on Malta was also strengthened with the arrival of additional aircraft. In an effort to reduce expected air operations against the convoy, airfields would be raided at Elmas and Decimomannu (Sardinia), at Pantelleria and Comiso (Sicily). At the end of July, the Tenth Submarine Flotilla had started to return to Malta. One of the first tasks would be to provide cover for 'Pedestal'.

The convoy passed through the Straits of Gibraltar under cover of darkness and on Tuesday the 11th, HMS *Furious* flew off the first batch of 38 Spitfires. One alighted again on *Indomitable* with mechanical problems, the remainder reached Malta. As this was taking place, the Royal Navy incurred its first casualty: HMS *Eagle* was hit by four torpedoes fired by *U.73*, sinking within eight minutes. Of nearly 1,100 on board, 927 were rescued.

In the early hours of the following morning, while returning westward with *Furious* on conclusion of 'Bellows', an escorting destroyer, *Wolverine*, rammed and sank the Italian submarine *Dagabur*. There were no survivors. Later that day, as the main force steamed east, another Italian submarine, *Cobalto*, was depth charged and forced to the surface, before being rammed by HMS *Ithuriel*; 41 of the submarine's crew were taken prisoner. Both destroyers were badly damaged *Ithuriel*, less so, but enough to impair her fighting efficiency.

Throughout the 12th, the force was covered by carrier-borne fighters, and there was an appearance in the evening by Beaufighters from Malta. There were three heavy air attacks on this date. Near misses left *Deucalion* with her speed reduced. That evening, the destroyer *Foresight* was struck by an Italian aerial torpedo (later having to be sunk by HMS *Tartar*) and *Indomitable* was hit by three bombs, rendering her flight deck unusable. The straggling *Deucalion* was further damaged and abandoned. On reaching the Skerki Channel, and slightly sooner than had been planned, the carrier withdrew with the remainder of Force Z, leaving Force X to continue with the merchant ships.

Towards nightfall, the cruiser *Nigeria* was struck by a torpedo fired by the Italian submarine *Axum*. Torpedoes from the same salvo hit HMS *Cairo* and *Ohio*. *Nigeria* remained afloat and would be escorted back to Gibraltar. The tanker was able to continue towards Malta, but *Cairo* could not be saved. *Empire Hope* and *Brisbane Star* were damaged in air attacks. *Clan Ferguson* received a direct hit and blew up and HMS *Kenya* was damaged by a torpedo from the Italian submarine *Alagi*.

'Pedestal' cost the Royal Navy and Merchant Navy dearly in human lives and shipping. This Luftwaffe aerial photograph was taken on 13 August 1942 and shows of the final moments of the merchantman *Waimarama*.

Greeted by crowds of jubilant Maltese, an escort vessel enters Grand Harbour on conclusion of 'Pedestal'.

Off Kelibia, Tunis, in the early hours of the 13th, there was a running fight with Italian and German torpedo boats, during which HMS *Manchester* was severely damaged (later scuttled); *Glenorchy* and *Wairangi* were sunk; *Almeria Lykes* and *Santa Elisa* were damaged and abandoned (the latter subsequently bombed and sunk). With daybreak, another merchant ship, *Waimarama*, was bombed, blowing up with heavy loss of life. Force X was now within range of Beaufighters and Spitfires from Malta. During continuing attacks *Ohio* and *Dorset* were immobilized. In the afternoon, warships from Malta arrived to escort the surviving merchant ships, enabling Force X to retire. *Penn*, *Ledbury* and *Bramham* remained with *Ohio* and *Dorset*. The latter was lost following further attacks.

Rochester Castle, *Melbourne Star* and *Port Chalmers* entered Grand Harbour in the evening of the 13th, followed by *Brisbane Star* the next afternoon. *Ohio* barely afloat, was eased into port in the morning of the 15th. Meanwhile, Force X had been targeted by enemy aircraft, but came through relatively unscathed to be met by Force Z, following which both forces withdrew to Gibraltar.

'Pedestal' had cost at least 450 Allied lives, mainly of the Merchant Navy, Royal Navy and Fleet Air Arm, Royal Marines and Maritime Regiment. Many more were injured and some had been taken prisoner. The RAF also suffered casualties, as did Italian and German aircrews and naval personnel.

At Malta, similar arrangements to those of June were put in force, some 3,000 army personnel joining local stevedores in the race to unload cargo. Enemy forces made no effort to bomb the ships at their moorings, By 23 August, 32,000 tons had been dispersed to dumps. In summarizing, the General Staff noted: 'The amounts received from the convoy will not be sufficient to cause any major alteration in the rations'. Although no one could have known at the time, it would be sufficient to sustain the island for the remainder of the siege.

AUTUMN 1942 AND THE FINAL AXIS OFFENSIVE

In early August, fighter pilots of 603 Squadron were absorbed by 229 Squadron which was reformed, this time as a Spitfire unit. On 17 August, HMS *Furious* flew off another batch of Spitfires (one pilot was lost in a take-off accident, two were rescued after baling out when their aircraft developed mechanical problems and one pilot was badly burned when he crashed on arriving at Luqa). In late July, bomb-carrying Hurricanes had carried out a raid on Sicily albeit with limited success. Offensive sorties were resumed on 20 August with FAA 'Hurri-bombers' and fighter sweeps by Spitfires.

In June, 75,467 tons of Axis supplies were handled at Benghazi, Tripoli and Derna, and, in July, a further 81,041 tons at Benghazi, Tripoli and Tobruk. The acquisition of naval barges and auxiliary sailing vessels helped the supply situation, particularly on coastal routes. But the continuing toll on shipping by Allied striking forces was still of concern for the Axis command. Malta-based Beauforts and escorting Beaufighters were especially successful in the second half of the month. The Italian merchantman *Rosolino Pilo* was damaged in an air attack during the night of 17/18 August and afterwards torpedoed and blown up the submarine *United* (*P 44*). On the 21st, the tanker *Pozarica* was damaged and subsequently beached at Corfu; on the 27th, in the eastern Mediterranean, the steamers *Dielpi* and *Istria* were lost as a result of air attacks and the troop transport

Manfredo Camperio was torpedoed by the submarine *Umbra* (*P 35*); off southern Italy, the tanker *Sanandrea* was bombed and set on fire on the 30th, sinking the next day. Notwithstanding these recent Allied successes, Axis supplies were still getting through. In August, shipping from Italy and the Aegean arrived with reinforcements and military supplies, including about 1,000 vehicles. A further 1,115 tons of materiel, together with 13,115 personnel arrived by air.

September was unusually quiet for Malta, with enemy air activity consisting of daylight fighter sweeps and very few night raids. Taking advantage of the situation, the RAF continued with offensive fighter sorties and striking forces maintained the pressure on Axis shipping. On 6 September, the German Naval Staff acknowledged 'the disturbingly large number' of ship losses. Submarines operating from Malta and bases at either end of the Mediterranean were especially successful, the Tenth Submarine Flotilla accounting for the Italian salvage vessel *Rostro* and auxiliary anti-submarine vessel *Giovanna* (both on the 17th), auxiliary minesweeper *Aquila*, a Vichy French steamer *Liberia* (21st), and the Italian *Leonardo Palomba* (22nd) and *Francesco Barbaro* (torpedoed on the 27th and lost while in tow). Nevertheless, nearly 1,200 vehicles and other supplies did get through, together with hundreds of reinforcements.

The majority of British shipping losses in the Mediterranean occurred mid-month mainly as a result of an unsuccessful amphibious assault in the Tobruk area (Operation 'Agreement'). Within days, the cruiser *Coventry*, destroyers *Sikh* and *Zulu* and several small craft were sunk. HM Submarine *Talisman* (*N 78*) was also lost while en route from Gibraltar to Malta.

October began much as September had ended. For the first time, some Spitfires were modified as fighter-bombers for raids on Sicilian airfields, where an increasing number of enemy bombers and fighters had been observed by aerial reconnaissance. Notwithstanding the decline in enemy air activity over Malta, the *Kriegsmarine* especially was still very much concerned about the ongoing disruption of Mediterranean supply routes and preparations were well in hand for a major air offensive.

On 11 October, the Luftwaffe and the Regia Aeronautica launched the first in a series of raids with bombers heavily escorted by fighters, five waves totalling some 60 Ju 88s targeting Malta's airfields. Attacks would continue in a similar vein for one week, day and night. But it was now very different from 1941, when air superiority had belonged to the Luftwaffe. There were now five Spitfire squadrons: 229 and 249 at Ta' Qali, 126 and 1435 at Luqa and 185 at Ħal Far. The RAF had learned from early mistakes, too, using improved fighter tactics and strategy. Enemy aircrews faced a daunting task. When possible, Spitfires met incoming raids before they could reach the coast. Bombers that got through faced more fighters and AA fire from hundreds of guns. After five days, the enemy employed a new tactic, attacking with many formations on a wide front and from several directions simultaneously. On the 18th, the Luftwaffe again changed tack. Losses had been heavy on both sides and it was evident that bombing alone was not the solution to problematic Malta. Daylight raids by Ju 88s were replaced by fighter sweeps and fighter-bomber attacks. These had a nuisance value but achieved little else.

Nearly all shipping losses in the Mediterranean in October were Italian merchantmen. Tenth Submarine Flotilla enjoyed one its most successful months. Attacks by *Safari* (*P 211*) resulted in severe damage to *Veglia* (on the 2nd) and *Eneo* (5th); during a subsequent patrol by *Safari*, the steamer *Titania*, already damaged by aircraft, was finished off by torpedo (20th). A boarding party from *Unbending* (*P 37*) used demolition charges to dispose of the requisitioned wine carrier *Lupa* (8th) and, next day, set fire to SS *Alga*. Another steamship, *Beppe*, and the destroyer, *Giovanni da Verrazzano* were torpedoed later in the month (19th). *Union* (*P 43*) torpedoed SS *Enrichetta* (10th). The following day, *Unruffled* (*P 46*) disposed of *Una* and, two days later, another steamship *Loreto*. The same day, a tanker, *Nautilus*, was despatched by HM Submarine *Utmost* (*N 19*) The last successes of the month were achieved by *Umbra* (*P 35*) with the torpedoing of the already-damaged SS *Amsterdam* and an accompanying tugboat, *Pronta* (23rd).

Notwithstanding the continuing effectiveness of Malta's striking forces, the Axis command now had other priorities. During the night of 23 October, the Allies launched a massive offensive at El Alamein in Egypt, finally halting Rommel. Operation 'Torch' followed, on 8 November, with landings by Anglo-American forces in French North Africa.

To help maintain Malta's defence, before the end of October, 29 Spitfires arrived from HMS *Furious*. There was still a shortage of provisions, however, nearly three months having passed since the arrival of 'Pedestal'. There had been supply runs by individual ships and submarines, but another convoy was urgently needed. On 12 November, HMS *Manxman* brought from Alexandria 350 tons of supplies, mostly foodstuffs, and about 100 army and RAF reinforcements. Six days later, HMS *Welshman* arrived from Algiers with a similar cargo and some 50 personnel of the Royal Electrical and Mechanical Engineers. Another convoy ('Stoneage') was also about to depart from the eastern Mediterranean. It would be covered by units of the Western Desert Air Force until west of Benghazi, from where Malta-based aircraft would take over. The Dutch merchantman *Bantam*, British *Denbighshire* and American *Mormacmoon* and *Robin Locksley* sailed from Port Said for the Mediterranean in the evening of 16 November. On the 18th, the convoy came under air attack. HMS *Arethusa* was struck by an aerial torpedo, resulting in some 200 casualties and putting the cruiser out of commission for more than a year. It was the only untoward event in an otherwise successful undertaking. The operation was concluded by the early hours of the 20th. 'Stoneage' fulfilled Malta's immediate supply needs and effectively brought an end to the siege, for while Axis air attacks would continue, these were to be on a much-reduced scale. The last heavy bombing raid, involving about 40 Ju 88s, was made during the night of 17/18 December 1942.

In April 1942, Malta was awarded the George Cross. But it was not until September before it was considered safe to hold a public ceremony at Palace Square, Valletta. Sir George Borg, seen here with Lord Gort, received the award on behalf of the people of Malta.

SUMMARY

The *Afrikakorps* was fought to a standstill and surrendered in Tunisia in May 1943, thereby shifting the balance of military power in the central Mediterranean and leaving it firmly in favour of the Allies. Two months later, Malta played a prominent role as Allied Headquarters and as a forward air base during Operation 'Husky' – the Allied invasion of Sicily.

Had the proposed Italo-German invasion of Malta gone ahead in 1942 and succeeded, as it almost certainly would have, things probably would have turned out very differently. The war in North Africa might well have ended with the surrender of British forces and with Suez and the oil-rich Middle East in Axis hands. What would then have been the stance of America, already heavily committed in its fight against Japan? With the way open for Italo-German forces to continue eastwards, potentially linking up with Japanese forces, Britain faced being rendered obsolete as a military power, leaving Hitler to concentrate on Russia.

Children amid the ruins in one of the Three Cities, probably Senglea, towards the end of 1942.

The ruins of St Augustine
Church in Valletta. The church
has since been rebuilt.

Residential areas, especially
those near military and
industrial targets, suffered
tremendous damage. Here,
rebuilding has commenced at
Senglea. But, in some areas,
bombsites remained for
decades after the war.

It is tempting to look back and discuss what might have happened 'if'. What if Mussolini had chosen to occupy Malta rather than Greece in 1940? What if Hitler had opted to seize Malta in mid-1941, in preference to Crete? The last real opportunity for invasion faded after mid-1942, by which time Axis forces had lost the initiative. Malta had defied the odds due, partly, to the unpreparedness and failure of Axis partners to take advantage of the island's weakened defences when the opportunity was there. In the end, Hitler's premature and overly optimistic decision to forego invasion, in the mistaken belief that, even with Malta in Allied hands, Axis forces would triumph in the Desert War, decided the island's fate. Malta, spared the ordeals of other, occupied, nations, remained undefeated.

THE BATTLEFIELD TODAY

Malta provided Britain with a military base until the withdrawal of Her Majesty's Forces in 1979. Until then, Pembroke served as the main barracks for rotating units of the army and Royal Marines. Military facilities were also maintained at Ħal Far, Ta' Qali, Kalafrana, Safi and Qrendi. Luqa was retained as the main RAF station, while a small civil airport was established at the eastern edge of the former wartime airfield. The site of what was RAF Luqa (including post-war family married quarters) has since been reclaimed and expanded to incorporate the modern Malta International Airport, as well as the Air Wing of the Armed Forces of Malta. All other airfields were eventually decommissioned. Ħal Far and Ta' Qali have both been

Post-war development has transformed Malta. In some rural settings, however, evidence of the war still remains. This is former HAA battery XHB 10.

redeveloped. The old RAF station at Kalafrana has been entirely demolished and replaced with a container terminal.

Some former military establishments were privatised. Pembroke is very different to what it was prior to the withdrawal of British Forces. A shopping mall and apartments have changed Tigné forever. Manoel Island, heavily bombed during 1941 and 1942, was left largely abandoned and derelict for decades, until a multi-million-euro facelift began to transform the area.

Throughout Malta, air raid shelters and underground installations remain, although in many cases, access is restricted or no longer possible. But numerous pillboxes, beach and defence posts and some HAA gun emplacements are still to be seen in mainly rural areas.

Grand Harbour, focus of so much attention during Italian and German air attacks, may from a distance appear much as it did before the destruction of so many of its buildings. But a closer inspection of surviving original architecture will reveal scars left by countless bomb splinters. After the July 1941 Italian attack, the harbour entrance was cleared of debris and the remaining bridge span removed. The breakwater remained unrepaired until the construction of a new pedestrian bridge, which was opened in 2012. Post-war, Grand Harbour remained a regular port of call for the Royal Navy, and later hosted visiting warships of the Sixth Fleet of the United States Navy. Today, the port caters for all kinds of merchant vessels, cruise ships and private yachts.

ACRONYMS AND ABBREVIATIONS

AA	Anti-Aircraft
AAG	Assistant Adjutant General
ADC	Aide-de-Camp
AMES	Air Ministry Experimental Station
AOC	Air Officer Commanding
A.S.	*Aerosiluranti* [torpedo bomber]
B.T.	*Bombardamento Terrestre* [bomber, land-based]
C-in-C	Commander-in-Chief
CoS	Chief of Staff
C.T.	*Caccia Terrestre* [fighter, land-based]
DAG	Deputy Assistant General
FAA	Fleet Air Arm
GOC	General Officer Commanding
HAA	Heavy Anti-Aircraft
HMAS	His Majesty's Australian Ship
HMS	His Majesty's Ship
HQ	Headquarters
HSL	High Speed launch
KOMR	King's Own Malta Regiment
LAA	Light Anti-Aircraft
ML	Motor Launch
MV	Merchant Vessel
OC	Officer Commanding
OR	Other Rank
PoW	Prisoner of War
RA	Royal Artillery
RAF	Royal Air Force
RASC	Royal Army Service Corps
RDF	Radio Direction Finding
RE	Royal Engineers
RFA	Royal Fleet Auxiliary
RFC	Royal Flying Corps
RMA	Royal Malta Artillery
RN	*Regia Nave*
RNAS	Royal Naval Air Service
R.S.T.	*Ricognizione Strategica Terrestre* [strategic reconnaissance, land-based]
T	Territorial
TA	Territorial Army
w.e.f.	with effect from

George 'Screwball' Beurling with the rudder and 'cat and mice' emblem of 378ª Squadriglia C.T. from sergente maggiore Faliero Gelli's shot-down Macchi C.202.

BIBLIOGRAPHY

Barnham, Denis, *One Man's Window: An Illustrated Account of Ten Weeks of War Malta, April 13th, to June 21st, 1942*, William Kimber (1956)

Beurling, Flying-Officer George F. D.S.O., D.F.C., D.F.M. and Bar, and Roberts, Leslie, *Malta Spitfire: The Story of a Fighter Pilot*, Hutchinson (1943)

Brennan, Pilot-Officer Paul D.F.C., D.F.M., Hesselyn, Pilot-Officer Ray D.F.M. and Bar, and Bateson, Henry, *Spitfires Over Malta*, Jarrolds (1943)

Caldwell, Donald, *The JG 26 War Diary, Volume One, 1939–42*, Grub Street (1996)

Cameron, Ian, *Red Duster, White Ensign: The Story of the Malta Convoys*, Frederick Muller (1959)

Debono, Charles, *Malta during World War II: The Strategic Role of the Island during the Conflict*, Book Distributors Limited (2017)

Fraser, Stanley, *The Guns of Ħaġar Qim: A Vivid Account of the Hazardous Life of a Gunner during World War Two: The Diaries of Stan Fraser 1939–1946*, Bieb Bieb Enterprises Ltd. (2005)

Hastings, Max, *Operation Pedestal: The Fleet that Battled to Malta 1942*, William Collins (2021)

Holland, James, *Fortress Malta: An Island under Siege, 1940–1943*, Orion Books Ltd. (2003)

Jackson, Bill, *Air Sea Rescue during the Siege of Malta: An Eyewitness Account of Life with HSL107 1941–43*, Matador (2010)

Johnston, Wing Commander Tim DFC, *Tattered Battlements: A Malta Diary by a Fighter Pilot*, Peter Davies (1943)

Lucas, Laddie, *Malta – The Thorn in Rommel's Side: Six Months that Turned the War*, Stanley Paul (1992)

Mahlke, Helmut, *Stuka, Angriff: Sturzfleug*, Verlag E.S. Mittler & Sohn (1993)

Malizia, Nicola, *Inferno su Malta: La Piú Lunga Battaglia Aeronavale della Seconda Guerra Mondiale*, Mursia (1976)

Neil, Wing Commander T. F. DFC*, AFC, AE, RAF Ret'd, *Onward to Malta: Memoirs of a Hurricane Pilot in Malta – 1941*, Airlife (1992)

Noppen, Ryan K., *Malta 1940–42: The Axis Air Battle for Mediterranean Supremacy*, Osprey Publishing Ltd (2018)

Prien, Jochen, *Jagdgeschwader 53: A History of the "Pik-As" Geschwader, March 1937 – May 1942*, Schiffer Publishing Ltd. (2004)

Prien, Jochen, *Jagdgeschwader 53: A History of the "Pik-As" Geschwader, May 1942 – January 1944*, Schiffer Publishing Ltd. (2004)

Prien, Jochen, *Geschichte des Jagdgeschwaders 77, Teil 3, 1942 – 1943*, Struve-Druck (1993)

Radtke, Siegfried, *Kampfgeschwader 54, Von der 52 zur Me 262, Eine Chronik nach Kriegstagebüchern, Berichten und Dokumenten, 1935–1945*, Schild Verlag (1990)

Rogers, Anthony, *185 The Malta Squadron*, Spellmount Limited. (1995)

Rogers, Anthony, *Air Battle of Malta: Aircraft Losses and Crash Sites 1940–42*, Greenhill Books (2017)

Rogers, Anthony, *Siege of Malta 1940–42*, Greenhill Books (2020)

Shankland, Peter and Hunter, Anthony, *Malta Convoy*, Collins (1961)

Shores, Christopher and Cull, Brian, with Malizia, Nicola, *Malta: The Hurricane Years 1940–41*, Grub Street (1987)

Shores, Christopher and Cull, Brian, with Malizia, Nicola, *Malta: The Spitfire Year 1942*, Grub Street (1991)

Smith, Peter, *Pedestal: The Malta Convoy of August 1942*, William Kimber (1970)

Stones, Donald, *Operation "Bograt" – From France to Burma* Spellmount (1990)

Vella, Philip, *Malta: Blitzed but not Beaten*, Progress Press (1985)

Wingate, John DSC, *The Fighting Tenth: The Tenth Submarine Flotilla and the Siege of Malta*, Leo Cooper (1991)

INDEX

Figures in **bold** refer to illustrations.

Aagtekirk, HMS 77
Abingdon, HMS 30, 64
Admiralty 6
Adriatico (transport) 47
air-sea rescue 54
aircraft, British 69, 76–77
    Blackburn Skua 15, 26, 28, 30
    Bristol Beaufighter 40
    Bristol Blenheim 15, 46, 51
    Fairey Fulmar 40–41
    Fairey Swordfish 23–24, 26, 28
    Gloster Sea Gladiator 6, 15, 23, 24–25
    Hawker Hurricane 15, 24, 25–26, 30, 33,
       35, 41, 51
    Martin Maryland 26
    Supermarine Spitfire 15, 58–59, 62, 70, 72, 81
    Vickers Wellington 29, 33, 51
aircraft, German 18, 30, 69, 72–73
    Ju 87; 32, 34, **36–37**, 38, **41**
    Ju 88; **33**, 34, 51–52
    Me Bf 109; 35, 39–40, 50, **52**, 59, 62
aircraft, Italian 18, 28
    Macchi C.202; **82–83**, 84
    S.79; 23, 24, 26, 29
aircraft, US:
    B-24 Liberator 77
Airedale, HMS 78
Airone (torpedo boat) 29
Ajax, HMS 29, 31, 53
Alagi (submarine) 85
Albania 20
Alexandria 17, 25, 27, 28, 29, 30
    and convoys 62–63
    and 'Excess' 31
Alga, SS 88
Almeria Lykes, HMS 81, 86
Alvise da Mosto (destroyer) 48
Amsterdam, SS 88
Ancient, HMS 64
Angeli, S.Cap Arnaldo de 76
anti-aircraft (AA) capabilities 6, 15, 23
Aquila (minesweeper) 87
Arethusa, HMS 78, 88
Argonauta (submarine) 25
Argus, HMS **15**, 25, 26, 30, 78, 81
Ariel (torpedo boat) 29
Ariosto (steamer) 54–55
Ark Royal, HMS 25, 26, 27, 28, 40–41, 46
    and 'Excess' 31
    and U-boats 47
Artigliere (destroyer) 29
Ashton, Sgt Dennis K. **27**
Aurora, HMS 46, 48
Avon Vale, HMS 64
Axum (submarine) 85

Badsworth, HMS 79–80
Bantam (merchantman) 88
Barham, HMS 30, 47
Beak, Col Daniel M. W. 10, 52
Beckett, Col Clifford T. 10
Bedouin, HMS 79
Benedetti, Mario 24
Beppe (steamer) 88
Berwick, HMS 30
Beryl, HMS 33, 74
Beurling, Sgt George 'Screwball' 76, 84, **93**
Bhutan, HMS 77
Birmingham, HMS 78
Bonaventure, HMS 31, **36–37**, 38
Bonham-Carter, Gen Sir Charles 9
Borg, Sir George **88**
Borg Pisani, S.Ten Carmelo 76
Bowerman, Sgt Oswald R. 'Drac' **27**
Brambleleaf, HMS 31
Bramham, HMS 86
Breconshire, HMS 31, 34, 40, 43, 53
    and 'M.W.10' 63, 64
Brisbane Star, HMS 81, 85, 86
British Army 6, 14–15, 17, 43, 46, 80
    and commanders 9–12
    1st Btn, Dorsetshire Rgt 24

Durham Light Infantry Rgt 53
Brook (steamer) 81
Burdwan, HMS 79
Burges, Flt Lt George 24

Cagna, Gen Stefano 26
Cairo, HMS 79, 81, 85
Calcutta, HMS 27, 28, 31
Cape Hawke, HMS 58
Carabelli, S.Ten Aristide 43
Carlisle, HMS 63
Cavallero, Gen Ugo 70
Centurion, HMS 78
Chant, HMS 79
Charybdis, HMS 81
Chiodi, Antonio 24
City of Calcutta, HMS 53, 77
Clan Campbell, HMS 63
Clan Cumming, HMS 31
Clan Ferguson, HMS 53, 81, 85
Clan Macaulay, HMS 31
Clan Macdonald, HMS 31
Clark, Lt Clifford 35
Cleopatra, HMS 63
Cobalto (submarine) 85
Comando Aeronautica Sicilia 18
Console Generale Liuzzi (submarine) 25
convoys 27–30, 31–34, 46–47, 62–64, 88
Cornwall, HMS 28
Cosulich, Ten Giuseppe 76
Coventry, HMS 27, 28, 87
Crete 31, 41, 77, 90
Cuma (steamship) 56
Cunningham, Adm Sir Andrew B. 25, 28, 32
Curteis, Vice Adm Alban T. B. 78
Cyrenaica 30, 77

Dagabur (submarine) 85
Dawson, WC Hugh L. **55**
Decoy, HMS 28, 33
Defender, HMS 31
Denbighshire, HMS 88
Desert War 19, 21, 40–41
Deucalion, HMS 85
Diamond, HMS 31
Diana (sloop) 42
Dielpi (steamer) 86
Dobbie, Lt-Gen Sir William G. S. 9, 70
Doglio, Capt Furio Niclot 84
Dorset, HMS 81, 86

E-Boats 18, 28
Eagle, HMS 25, 28, 29, 40, 78, 85
    and Spitfires 58, 62, 70, 72, 81
East Africa 19
Eddy, HMS 75
Egypt 19, 21, 30, 88; *see also* Alexandria
Elizabeth Bakke, HMS 77
Empire Hope, HMS 81, 85
Empire Song, HMS 31
Eneo (merchantman) 88
Enigma 46–47, 55
Enrichetta, SS 88
Eridge, HMS 63
Espero (destroyer) 25
Essex, HMS 31, 32, 33, 34
Euralyus, HMS 63

Fearless, HMS 43
Fellers, Col Bonner F. 65, 69
Firedrake, HMS 43
Fleet Air Arm (FAA) 23
    800X Sqn 40–41
Ford, Vice Adm Sir Wilbraham T. R. 10, 52
Foresight, HMS 85
France 6, 23
Francesco Barbaro (cargo vessel) 87
Furious, HMS 40, 81, 85, 86, 88

Galatea, HMS 48
Gallant, HMS 32, 34, 64
Geisler, GendF Hans Ferdinand 13
Gelli, Sgt Mag Faliero 84
George VI of Britain, King 65

Germany 20; *see also* Hitler, Adolf
Gibraltar 21, 24, 27, 28, 31, 58
Giovanna (anti-submarine vessel) 87
Giovanni da Verrazzano (destroyer) 88
Giovanni delle Bande Nere (cruiser) 63, 64
Glasgow, HMS 30
Glengyle, HMS 53
Glenorchy, HMS 85, 86
Gloucester, HMS 25, 28, 29, 31, 32
Göring, Hermann 13
Gorizia (heavy cruiser) 63
Gort, John Vereker, Lord 9–10, 70, **88**
Grand Harbour 20, **21**, 56, 85
    and attacks 23, **36–37**, 38–39, 65
    and Italian attacks 42–43, **44–45**
Great Britain 6, 21
Greece 20, 30, 40, 90; *see also* Crete
Guglielmo, Giuseppe 76
Gurkha, HMS 53

Hal Far 6, 15, **20**, 23, 91–92
    and Hurricane squadrons 59
    and RAF 51
Hardy, Capt Cecil C. 78
Hartley, Flt Lt Peter 24–25
Harwood, Vice Adm Sir Henry 77
Hasty, HMS 77
Hatcher, Corp George **35**
Havock, HMS 63, 64–65
Hebe, HMS 79, 80
Heppell, Flt Lt Philip 59
Hereward, HMS 32
Hermione, HMS 78
Hero, HMS 27
Heythrop, HMS 63
Hitler, Adolf 20, 40, 50, 70, 90
Hostile, HMS 27
Hotspur, HMS 77
Hyperion, HMS 30

Ilex, HMS 28, 31
Illustrious, HMS 27, 28, 29, 30, 31
    and 'Blitz' **32**, 33, 34, 35
Imperial, HMS 29
Imperial Star, HMS 43
India 19
Indomitable, HMS 81, 85
Iridio Mantovani (tanker) 47
Istria (steamer) 86
Italian Navy *see* Regia Marina
Italy 6, 19–20, 21, 35; *see also* Sardinia; Sicily
Ithuriel, HMS 85

Janus, HMS 27, 31
Japan 89
Jervis, HMS 48
Jolly, Lt David R. H. 73
Justified, HMS 80

Kalafrana 6, 23, 51, 59, 91, 92
Kandahar, HMS 48
Keeble, Flt Lt Peter 24
Kelsey, Sgt Eric N. **27**
Kemnade, Kaptlt Friedrich 56, 58, 73, 74
Kent, HMS 28
Kentucky, HMS 79
Kenya, HMS 81, 85
Kesselring, GenFM Albert 12–13, 20, 48, 50,
    54, 70
Kingston, HMS 63, 64, 65
Krahl, Hptm Karl-Heinz 59
Kujawiak (destroyer) 80

Lalli, Gen Gennaro Tedeschini 12
Lance, HMS 46, 64
Lanciere (destroyer) 63
Lazzaretto 20, 54
Leatham, Vice Adm Sir Ralph 10, **11**, 52
Leckie, Air Cmdre Robert 11
Ledbury, HMS 86
Legion, HMS 63–64
Leibing, Fw Werner 35
Leonardo Palomba (steamer) 87
Leone Pancaldo (destroyer) 25

Liberia (steamer) 87
Libya 19, 20, 21, 25, 30
  and convoys 27, 69, 73
  and German Army 80
  and '*Maestrale*' 46–47
  and supplies 46, 86
Littorio (battleship) 63, 77
Lively, HMS 46, 63
Liverpool, HMS 25, 28, 29, 78
Lloyd, AVM Hugh Pughe 11, 41, 81
Loerzer, Genlt Bruno 13, 50
Loreto (steamer) 88
Luftwaffe **22**, 33–34, 48, 50–56, **60–61**, 87
  II.Fliegerkorps 18, 50, 62
  X.Fliegerkorps 18, 20, 30
  7./Jagdgeschwader 26 35, 39, 40, 41
  7.Flieger-Dvn 70
  see also aircraft, German
Lupa (wine carrier) 88
Luqa airfield 6, 15, **20**, 29
  and attacks **39**, 51
  and RAF 26, 91

McAdam, PO Allan 24
'*Maestrale*' convoy 46–47
Malaya, HMS 28, 31
Malta Night Fighter Unit (MNFU) 41
Malta Police 77
Manchester, HMS **42**, 43, 81, 86
Manfredo Camperio (troop transport) 86–87
Manxman, HMS 88
Maori, HMS 54, 55
maps:
  heavy anti-aircraft gun positions 75
  HMS *Welshman* supplies **71**
  infantry sectors (May/June 1940) **16**
  light anti-aircraft gun positions 78
  Luftwaffe operations **60–61**
  Malta infantry brigade areas 74
  Mediterranean (1940) **4**
  minefields 57
  minelaying operations 57
  RAF and Axis airfields **22**
  searchlight positions 79
Marigold, HMS 47
Matchless, HMS 79–80
Mayall, Sgt Jack 59
Maynard, Air Cmdre Forster H. M. 11, 41
Mazzucco, Gen Renato 12
Melbourne Star, HMS 85, 86
Middle East 19, 89
minefields 57
minelaying 56, **57**, 58, 73–75
Mirschinka, Uffz Werner 52
Moccagatta, Capt Vittorio 42, 43
Mohawk, HMS 27
Mormacmoon, USS 88
MTSMs 75–76
Müncheberg, Oblt Joachim 35
Murray, PO Ken 59
Mussolini, Benito **13**, 17, 20, 50, 90

Nautilus, HMS 88
Nelson, HMS 43, 81
Neptune, HMS 48
Nestor, HMS 78
Newcastle, HMS 30, 77
Nigeria, HMS 81, 85
North Africa 19, 20, 21, 35; *see also* Desert War;
  Egypt; Libya; Tunisia
Northern Prince, HMS 31
Norwell, Sgt John K. 'Angus' **40**
Nubian, HMS 27

O'Donnell, Sgt Roy **15**
Ohio, HMS 85, 86
Olympus, HMS (submarine) 75
operations:
  'C3'/'*Herkules*' (1942) 70
  'Calendar' (1942) 69
  'Colossus' (1941) 34–34
  'Excess' (1941) 31–34
  'Halberd' (1941) 43
  'Hurray' (1940) **15**, 25–27
  'Husky' (1943) 89
  'Julius' (1942) 76–80

'M.F.3' (1942) 53
'Pedestal' (1942) 81, 85–86
'Status II' (1941) 46
'Substance' (1941) 42–43
'Vigorous' (1942) 77
Orari, HMS 79, 81
Orion, HMS 28, 31, 32

Pampas, HMS 63, 64
Pandora, HMS 64
Park, AVM Sir Keith R. 11–12, 81
Parramatta, HMAS 47
Partridge, HMS 79
Pedretti, 2C Alcide 43
Penelope, HMS 46, 48, 63, 64, 65
Penn, HMS 86
Perth, HMAS 31, 32, 33
Perthshire, HMS 39
Phoebe, HMS 81
Pia, S.Cap Aldo 76
Plumleaf, HMS 27–28, 64
Port Chalmers, HMS 81, 86
Pozarica (tanker) 86
Price-Fox, 1Lt Frederick 73
Primula, HMS 77
Pronta (tugboat) 88

Queen Elizabeth, HMS 48

radar 6, 15, 17, 42–43
Raeder, Grossadm Erich 70
Rahlmeier, Fw Heinz 59
Raimondo Montecuccoli (cruiser) 79
Regia Aeronautica 17–18, 21, 23, 40, 50–51, 87
  and airfields **22**
  and 'C3' 70
  and Grand Harbour attacks 42
Regia Marina 18, 25, 28, 56, 63, 75–76
  and Grand Harbour attacks 42–43, **44–45**
Reichenfels (steamer) 80
Renown, HMS 27, 31
Richter, Oblt Gerhard 34
Robin Locksley, USS 88
Rochester Castle, HMS 81, 86
Rodney, HMS 81
Romania 20
Rommel, Genlt Erwin 35, 53, 70, 88
Rosolino Pilo (merchantman) 86
Rostro (salvage vessel) 87
Royal Air Force (RAF) 6, 15, 20, 23, 27
  and airfields **22**
  and Grand Harbour 39
  see also aircraft, British
Royal Air Force (RAF) (units):
  37 Sqn 56
  46 Sqn 41
  126 Sqn 41
  148 Sqn 29
  229 Sqn 86
  242 Sqn 47
  249 Sqn 41, 55
  252 Sqn 40
  258 Sqn 47
  261 Sqn 26, **27**, 40
  605 Sqn 47
Royal Australian Navy 40
Royal Navy 6, 15, 17, 20, 23, 25, 40
rubble wall camouflage 53
Rubino (submarine) 25

Safari, HMS 88
Sagona, HMS 48
St Angelo, HMS 75
Sanandrea (tanker) 87
Santa Elisa, HMS 81, 86
Sardinia 18, 26, 46, 51
Savona (steamer) 81
Scaroni, Gen Silvio 12, 50
Schnellboote 56, **57**, 58
  3.Schnellbootflottille 18, 73–75, 77
Schnez, Oblt Viktor 52
Scirocco (destroyer) 63
Scobell, Maj-Gen Sir S. J. P. (John) 10, 52
Scobie, Maj-Gen Ronald MacK. 10–11
seaplanes 6
Sheffield, HMS 27, 31

Sicily 18, 20, 21, 30
  and air operations 46
  and airfields 70
  and convoys 27
  and German Army 80
  and invasion 89
  and Luftwaffe 50
  and Palermo Harbour 56
  and Regia Aeronautica 40
Sikh, HMS 87
Sikorski, Gen Władysław **9**
Sirius, HMS 81
Sirte, Second Battle of (1942) **54**
Somerville, Vice Adm James F. 25, 31
Southampton, HMS 31, 32
Southwold, HMS 64
Soviet Union 40
Stuart, HMAS 31
Sturla (steamer) 81
submarines 20, 25, 27, 64; *see also* E-Boats;
  U-boats
Suez Canal 19, 21, 89
Sunset, HMS 64
Sydney, HMAS 28, 31
Sydney Star, HMS 43
Syfret, Vice Adm Edward N. 81

Ta' Qali airfield 6, **21**, 41, 51, 59, 91–92
  and bombing **82–83**, 84
Talabot, HMS 63, 64
Talisman, HMS 81
Tanimbar (cargo ship) 78
Tedder, AM Sir Arthur W. 77
Tembien (steamer) 55
Terror, HMS 30
Tesei, Mag Teseo 43
Thermopylae, M/S 53
Timms, Sgt W. J. (Bill) **15**
torpedinieri 29
torpedoes **19**, 75–76
Tovey, Vice Adm John C. 28
Trento (heavy cruiser) 77
Troilus, HMS 79, 81
Trusty Star, HMS 74, 79
Tunisia 19, 29, 55, 86, 89
Turner, Sqn Ldr P.S. (Stan) 55–56

U-boats 47–48
Uebi Scebeli (submarine) 25
Ugolino Vivaldi (destroyer) 79
Umbra, HMS (submarine) 77, 87, 88
Unbeaten, HMS 64
Unbending, HMS 88
Ungarelli, S.Ten Ongarillo 76
United States of America (USA) 65, 69, 89
Unruffled, HMS 88
Upholder, HMS 65

Valiant, HMS 27, 28, 31, 48
Valletta 55
Vega (torpedo boat) 31–32
Veglia (merchantman) 88
Vendetta, HMAS 30
Verdala barracks 23
Vian, Rear Adm Philip L. 63, 77–78
Victoria (transport) 53–54
Victorious, HMS 81
Volo, HMS 28

Waimarama, HMS 81, 85, 86
Wairangi, HMS 81, 86
Warspite, HMS 28, 31
Wasp, USS 69, 70
Watson, Flt Lt Gerald 35
Wavell, Gen Sir Archibald P. 40
Welshman, HMS **71**, 72, 74, 76, 78, 88
Wolverine, HMS 85
Woodhall, Grp Capt A. B. 'Woody' 55–56

XHB 8 66–67, 68
XHB 10 68, 77, 91

York, HMS 31

Zulu, HMS 87